National Curriculum

ENGLISH

Teacher's

PLANNING & ASSESSMENT GUIDE

Year 2

Key Stage 1

Scholastic Education, an imprint of Scholastic Ltd
Book End, Range Road, Witney, Oxfordshire, OX29 0YD
Registered office: Westfield Road, Southam, Warwickshire CV47 0RA
www.scholastic.co.uk

1 2 3 4 5 6 7 8 9   6 7 8 9 0 1 2 3 4 5

British Library Cataloguing-in-Publication Data
A catalogue record for this book is available from the British Library.

ISBN 978-1407-16017-7

Printed and bound by Ashford Colour Press

Author Charlotte Raby
Editorial Rachel Morgan, Jenny Wilcox, Catherine Allison, Suzanne Adams
Cover and Series Design Neil Salt and Nicolle Thomas
Layout Tracey Camden
CD-ROM Development Hannah Barnett, Phil Crothers and MWA
Technologies Private Ltd

Recommended system requirements:

Windows: XP (Service Pack 3), Vista (Service Pack 2), Windows 7,
Windows 8 and Windows 10 with 2.33GHz processor
Mac: OS 10.6 to 10.10 with Intel Core™ Duo processor
1GB RAM (recommended)
1024 x 768 Screen resolution
CD-ROM drive (24x speed recommended)
Adobe Reader (version 9 recommended for Mac users)
Microsoft Word

For all technical support queries (including no CD drive), please phone Scholastic
Customer Services on 0845 6039091.

Table of Contents Year 2

About the Planning and Assessment Guides

Scholastic National Curriculum English scheme provides schools and teachers with a flexible scheme of work to meet all of your needs for the English curriculum, allowing you to keep control of what you teach, and when, while saving precious teacher time.

The scheme consists of four components:

- Teacher's *Planning and Assessment Guide*
- Children's *Textbook*
- *100 English Lessons* resource books and CD-ROMs
- Children's *English Practice Book*

The main benefits of the programme include:

- Accessible content geared towards the demands of the National Curriculum.
- Flexibility to fit into the way you already teach using the award-winning *100 English Lessons* teacher's books.
- Detailed support in the *Textbooks* to build secure foundations and deep understanding of key concepts.
- A bank of well-structured exercises in the *practice books* linked to clear explanations, which parents can understand and use to help their children.

Using the Planning and Assessment Guide

This book provides guidance on how to introduce topics (including how quickly) and how to support and extend the content in the *Textbook*. It references the accompanying *100 English Lessons* and *Practice Books* so you can use this material to further support learning. Each teaching notes page uses the same heading structure:

- **Prior learning:** details what the children should already know prior to introducing this content.
- **Curriculum objectives and Success criteria:** provides information about which National Curriculum objectives the section covers and the specific success criteria which will come from it.
- **Learn:** relates to the 'Learn' heading in the *Textbook*, but it also goes beyond this and helps you to introduce the learning appropriately.
- **Talk:** provides speaking and listening activities, where relevant.
- **Activities:** gives pointers for those activities in the *Textbook*, as well as giving ideas to extend or support the learning.
- **Write:** provides writing activities to further develop the learning, where relevant.
- *100 English Lessons* and *Practice Book* **links:** these detail related lessons and activities that you can use to enhance and further develop the teaching and learning of the subject area.

Planning and Assessment CD-ROM

The accompanying CD-ROM contains planning and assessment tools, the majority of these have been supplied as a word document so you can edit them to meet your needs. They can be used as effective tools for monitoring performance, identifying areas of weakness and communicating to parents.

Tracking progress

- **English progression overview:** gives an overview of the whole English curriculum across Years 1–6.
- **Teacher tracking:** breaks down an individual year group into three stages of progress 'working towards', 'working at expected level' and 'working at greater depth'.
- **Child progress chart:** 'I can' statements related to the *Textbook*. The children tick to show whether they are 'not sure', are 'getting there' or 'have got' a concept.
- **I can statements:** a cut-out format of the 'I can' statements from the child progress chart.

Planning and reporting templates

For templates – see the template menu on the CD-ROM.

- **Yearly, Termly and Weekly planning:** plan your teaching – templates and completed samples.
- **Termly report:** feed back to parents – templates and completed samples.

Other resources

- **Assessment framework for English:** printable DfE Interim Teacher Assessment frameworks for English
- **Curriculum links:** printable version of the curriculum links found on pages 7–9 of this book.
- **Glossary:** printable version of a child-friendly and age-appropriate English glossary.

Planning with Scholastic English

This series is arrange at a topic level (grammar, spelling, reading, writing) to provide discreet guidance on how to cover the different aspects of the National Curriculum. It is not intended that you would teach this content in a linear fashion, but instead use the content provided to support existing planning or develop new planning incorporating it.

The table on pages 7–9 of this book provides the curriculum objectives with page references to the *Textbook*, *100 English Lessons* and *Practice Book* to assist your planning. There is one omission to this grid, handwriting objectives have not been included due to varied handwriting policies within schools. Handwriting is part of the National Curriculum and provision should be included for this in your planning, both in focussed sessions and throughout general classwork.

About the Textbooks

Using the Textbooks

The *Textbook* and *Planning and Assessment Guide* are arranged thematically and are completely in line with the National Curriculum, allowing teachers and English subject leaders to create long- and medium-term plans best suited to the school's needs. Each section of the *Textbook* presents the 'core' learning for that curriculum area, with the relevant pages in the *Planning and Assessment Guide* providing further advice and links to additional lessons and resources, in particular to *100 English Lessons* and *English Practice Book*.

Textbook structure

Each section has a similar structure.

- **Learn:** examples and facts specific to the objective in question.
- **Tips:** short and simple advice to aid understanding.
- **Activities:** a focused range of questions, with answers provided in the *Planning and Assessment Guide*.

Remember that the *Planning and Assessment Guide* provides advice and links for extending learning and practice in each of these areas.

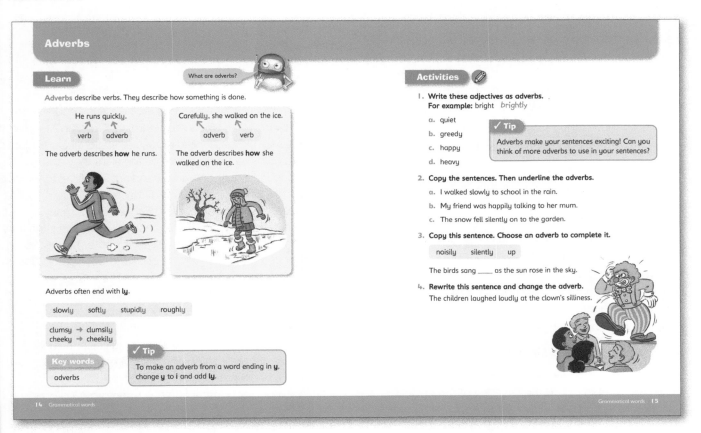

Tracking progress

Assessment is always an ongoing process – formative assessments provide feedback to teacher and child for next steps; summative assessment provides snapshots of a child's current competence.

There is a self-assessment chart for children on the CD-ROM (Child progress chart). This is intended as a method of engaging children in considering their own achievement; it might also be referenced by teachers in making their own judgements. Each 'I can' statement is a generalisation for each section in the *Textbook*. These statements are also provided in a cut-out and stick format.

The CD-ROM also provides a progression overview document – summarising the progress between year groups and a teacher tracking grid that allows you to track more detailed progress within a year group. The teacher tracking grid breaks each curriculum objective down into working towards the expected standard, working at the expected standard or working with greater depth. Each of these terms is explained below.

Working towards the expected standard

At this stage, children are able to access the objective at a simple level, or with some kind of support, whether from an adult, a peer or via some form of supportive resource. Children requiring support to complete work may:

- read a some texts for different purposes and demonstrate some understanding of these with support.
- write texts with emerging skills.
- can write for a purpose and audience only when scaffolding is provided.
- have difficulty correcting mistakes.

Working at the expected standard

Children working at the expected level on an English objective will be able to fulfil the essence of the objective independently. Indications that children are working at the expected standard for a particular objective include:

- read and demonstrate understanding of a wide range of age-appropriate texts for a range of purposes.
- write good-quality texts.
- demonstrate some understanding of purpose and audience in their writing.
- correct their own mistakes in work marked by others.

Working at greater depth

This category suggests that children have mastered the objective involved. They can demonstrate the skills used independently in a range of context. Indicators that children are working at greater depth include:

- read and demonstrate understanding of more demanding texts for a range of purposes.
- write longer, better-quality texts.
- demonstrate an understanding of purpose and audience when writing.
- spot errors and self-correct them.

DFE interim guidance (2015) on English assessment is available on the CD-ROM.

Scholastic English and Mastery

There are many definitions of 'mastery' in English. As well as judging how much a child has learned, it is important to assess how well they apply their learning. Children's English knowledge should be applied across all National Curriculum areas, this helps to give purpose to the skills they are learning and help deepen understanding. The level to which they can do this is one definition of mastery.

Scholastic National Curriculum English offers many opportunities for children to demonstrate using the skills they have learned. The *100 English Lessons* content provides content based around children's books to develop children's learning. To deepen or embed these skills the *English Practice Books* and *Textbooks* offer a range of well-structured exercises. The range of opportunities within the programme to embed or apply English skills therefore should provide teachers with sufficient evidence to track how secure English concepts are and whether they have truly been mastered by each child.

An individual report template has been provided on the CD-ROM to feed back to parents how well their child can apply their skills that they have learned. This might be done termly or at other times when children have attained a secure level of mastery in a particular area.

Curriculum objectives	Year 2 Textbook	100 English Lessons Year 2	Year 2 Practice Book
Word recognition			
Note, specific coverage has not been provided for these objectives as it is assumed that they will be covered as part of other teaching areas: • To continue to apply phonic knowledge and skills as the route to decode words until automatic decoding has become embedded and reading is fluent. • To read accurately by blending the sounds in words that contain the graphemes taught so far, especially recognising alternative sounds for graphemes. • To read accurately words of two or more syllables that contain the same graphemes as above. • To read words containing common suffixes. • To read further common exception words, noting unusual correspondences between spelling and sound and where these occur in the word. • To read most words quickly and accurately, without overt sounding and blending, when they have been frequently encountered. • To read aloud books closely matched to their improving phonic knowledge, sounding out unfamiliar words accurately, automatically and without undue hesitation. • To re-read these books to build up their fluency and confidence in word reading.			
Reading comprehension			
Note, specific coverage has not been provided for these objectives as it is assumed that they will be covered as part of other teaching areas: • To listen to, discuss and express views about a wide range of contemporary and classic poetry, stories and non-fiction at a level beyond that at which they can read independently. • To become increasingly familiar with and retell a wider range of stories, fairy stories and traditional tales. • To answer and ask questions.			
To discuss the sequence of events in books and how items of information are related.	Pages: 54–55	Pages: 20, 61, 86, 156, 158, 166, 189, 192	Pages: 100–101, 104–105, 116–117
To be introduced to non-fiction books that are structured in different ways.	Pages: 56–57	Pages: 26, 60, 61, 93, 123, 134, 154, 182	Pages: 100–101, 104–105, 116–117
To recognise simple recurring literary language in stories and poetry.	Pages: 68–69	Pages: 22, 52, 115, 116, 130, 131	Pages: 102–103
To discuss and clarify the meanings of words, linking new meanings to known vocabulary.	Pages: 58–59	Pages: 35, 53, 66, 188	Pages: 62, 108–109
To discuss their favourite words and phrases.	Pages: 66–67	Pages: 19, 30, 34, 84, 98, 117, 131, 150, 151, 190	
To continue to build up a repertoire of poems learned by heart, appreciating these and reciting some, with appropriate intonation to make the meaning clear.		Pages: 34, 66, 67, 68, 98, 130, 185, 186, 187	
To draw on what they already know or on background information and vocabulary provided by the teacher.	Pages: 58–59, 64–65	Pages: 20, 24, 26, 32, 51, 83, 90, 91, 148, 157, 158, 183, 191, 193	Pages: 62, 106–107, 108–109, 114–115
To check that the text makes sense to them as they read and to correct inaccurate reading.	Pages: 66–67	Pages: 26, 27, 52, 166, 179	
To make inferences on the basis of what is being said and done.	Pages: 64–65	Pages: 19, 20, 24, 52, 54, 55, 63, 64, 85, 87, 102, 117, 118, 119, 124, 126, 128, 156, 179, 180, 189, 190	Pages: 106–107, 114–115
To predict what might happen on the basis of what has been read so far.	Pages: 62–63	Pages: 19, 38, 84, 115, 156, 188	Pages: 112–113
To participate in discussion about books, poems and other works that are read to them and those that they can read for themselves, taking turns and listening to what others say.	Pages: 54–55	Pages: 21, 24, 31, 32, 34, 54, 55, 60, 62, 83, 84, 86, 92, 93, 100, 118, 119, 121, 124, 126, 128, 188	
To explain and discuss their understanding of books, poems and other material, both those that they listen to and those that they read for themselves.	Pages: 60, 61, 62–63	Pages: 30, 56, 61, 84, 116, 124, 153, 158	Pages: 100–101, 106–107, 112–113, 114–115
Transcription – Spelling			
Note, specific coverage has not been provided for these objectives as it is assumed that they will be covered as part of other teaching areas: • To segment spoken words into phonemes and representing these by graphemes, spelling many correctly. • To write from memory simple sentences dictated by the teacher that include words using the GPCs, common exception words and punctuation taught so far.			
To learn new ways of spelling phonemes for which one or more spellings are already known, and learn some words with each spelling, including a few common homophones.	Pages: 33, 34, 50–51	Pages: 67, 68, 99, 122, 186, 187	Pages: 15, 25, 26, 29, 33, 48, 49, 50, 51
To learn to spell common exception words.	Pages: 48	Pages: 58, 66, 157, 194, 197	Pages: 52–58
To learn to spell more words with contracted forms.	Pages: 24–25	Pages: 23, 32, 125, 157, 181, 196	
To learn the possessive apostrophe (singular).	Pages: 26–27	Pages: 87, 157, 158, 159, 160, 163, 165, 196	Pages: 44, 45, 96, 97
To distinguish between homophones and near-homophones.	Pages: 50–51	Pages: 99, 186, 187, 194	Pages: 48, 49, 50, 51

Curriculum objectives	Year 2 Textbook	100 English Lessons Year 2	Year 2 Practice Book
To add suffixes to spell longer words, including 'ment', 'ness', 'ful', 'less', 'ly'.	Pages: 28–29	Pages: 90, 96, 101, 125, 133, 195	Pages: 36, 37, 38, 39, 59, 61, 62, 63–64
To spell the /dj/ sound spelled as 'ge' and 'dge' at the end of words, and sometimes spelled as 'g' elsewhere in words before 'e', 'i' and 'y'. (Spelling appendix)	Pages: 38	Pages: 87, 163	Pages: 6, 7
To spell the /s/ sound spelled 'c' before 'e', 'i' and 'y'. (Spelling appendix)	Pages: 40	Pages: 14	Pages: 8
To spell the /n/ sound spelled 'kn' and (less often) 'gn' at the beginning of words. (Spelling appendix)	Pages: 39	Pages: 14, 122	Pages: 9, 10
To spell the /r/ sound spelled 'wr' at the beginning of words. (Spelling appendix)	Pages: 39	Pages: 14, 122	Pages: 9, 10
To spell the /l/ or /ul/ sound spelled 'le', 'el' and 'al' at the end of words. (Spelling appendix)	Pages: 36–37	Pages: 14	Pages: 11, 12, 13, 14
To spell words ending 'il'. (Spelling appendix)	Pages: 36–37	Pages: 14	Pages: 11, 12, 13, 14
To spell the /igh/ sound spelled 'y' at the end of words. (Spelling appendix)	Pages: 42		Pages: 15
To add 'es' to nouns and verbs ending in 'y'. (Spelling appendix)	Pages: 52–53		Pages: 16, 17, 18
To add 'ed', 'ing', 'er' and 'est' to a root word ending in 'y' with a consonant before it. (Spelling appendix)	Pages: 30–31	Pages: 13, 127, 151	Pages: 19, 20, 21, 22, 23, 24, 59
To add 'ing', 'ed', 'er', 'est' and 'y' to words ending in 'e' with a consonant before it. (Spelling appendix)	Pages: 30–31	Pages: 13, 127, 151	Pages: 19, 20, 21, 22, 23, 24, 59
To add 'ing', 'ed', 'er', 'est' and 'y' to words of one syllable ending in a single consonant after a single vowel. (Spelling appendix)	Pages: 30–31	Pages: 13, 127, 151	Pages: 19, 20, 21, 22, 23, 24, 59
To spell the /or/ sound spelled 'a' before 'l' and 'll'. (Spelling appendix)	Pages: 44		Pages: 25, 26
To spell the /u/ sound spelled 'o'. (Spelling appendix)	Pages: 45		Pages: 27, 28
To spell the /ee/ sound spelled 'ey'. (Spelling appendix)	Pages: 43	Pages: 14	Pages: 29
To spell the /o/ sound spelled 'a' after 'w' and 'qu'. (Spelling appendix)	Pages: 35	Pages: 14	Pages: 30, 31
To spell the /ur/ sound spelled 'or' after 'w'. (Spelling appendix)	Pages: 46–47	Pages: 14	Pages: 32, 33
To spell the /or/ sound spelled 'ar' after 'w'. (Spelling appendix)	Pages: 46–47	Pages: 14	Pages: 32, 33
To spell the /zh/ sound spelled 's'. (Spelling appendix)	Pages: 41		Pages: 34, 35
To spell words ending in 'tion'. (Spelling appendix)	Pages: 32		Pages: 46, 47

Composition

Note, specific coverage has not been provided for these objectives as it is assumed that they will be covered as part of other teaching areas:
* To evaluate their writing with the teacher and other pupils.
* To read aloud what they have written with appropriate intonation to make the meaning clear.

To write narratives about personal experiences and those of others (real and fictional).	Pages: 70–71	Pages: 58, 63, 64, 65, 88, 158, 160, 161, 163, 167, 182, 191, 193	Pages: 118
To write about real events.	Pages: 72–73	Pages: 90, 96, 155	Pages: 123
To write poetry.	Pages: 74–75	Pages: 36, 100, 131, 132, 152, 187	Pages: 124, 125
To write for different purposes.	Pages: 76–77	Pages: 20, 21, 26, 27, 29, 30, 33, 39, 62, 94, 120, 126, 129, 149, 154, 155	Pages: 122, 126, 127
To plan or say out loud what they are going to write about.	Pages: 70–71, 72–73, 74–75, 76–77	Pages: 29, 33, 36, 57, 58, 61, 88, 89, 90, 95, 96, 99, 103, 120, 123, 158, 159, 160, 161, 162, 183, 192, 193, 199	Pages: 118, 122, 123, 124, 125, 126, 127
To write down ideas and/or key words, including new vocabulary.	Pages: 70–71, 72–73, 74–75, 76–77	Pages: 21, 28, 32, 35, 39, 52, 53, 55, 56, 58, 61, 71, 99, 118, 120, 122, 123, 126, 153, 154, 159, 160, 161, 182, 183, 192	Pages: 118, 122, 123, 124, 125, 126, 127
To encapsulate what they want to say, sentence by sentence.	Pages: 70–71, 72–73, 74–75, 76–77	Pages: 29, 64, 65, 88, 99, 103, 120, 123, 162, 183, 195, 199	Pages: 118, 122, 123, 124, 125, 126, 127
To re-read to check that their writing makes sense and that verbs to indicate time are used correctly and consistently, including ly verbs in the continuous form.	Pages: 78–79	Pages: 58, 59, 62, 63, 65, 91, 135, 184, 195. 196	

Curriculum objectives	Year 2 Textbook	100 English Lessons Year 2	Year 2 Practice Book
To proofread to check for errors in spelling, grammar and punctuation.	Pages: 80	Pages: 29, 58, 59, 91, 135, 164, 184	
Vocabulary, grammar and punctuation			
To learn how to use both familiar and new punctuation correctly (see English Appendix 2), including full stops, capital letters, exclamation marks, question marks, commas for lists and apostrophes for contracted forms and the possessive (singular).	Pages: 20–21, 22–23, 24–25, 26–27	Pages: 20, 23, 24, 27, 28, 31, 32, 36, 58, 59, 69, 125, 163, 164, 181, 182, 184, 196, 199	Pages: 44, 45, 67, 68, 69, 70, 71, 72, 73, 86, 87, 88, 90, 91, 92, 93, 96, 97
To use sentences with different forms: statement, question, exclamation, command.	Pages: 20–21	Pages: 23, 24, 26, 27, 28, 69, 93, 94, 116, 133, 195, 196, 199	Pages: 67, 68, 69, 70, 71, 72, 73, 86, 87, 88
To use expanded noun phrases to describe and specify.	Pages: 9	Pages: 25, 32, 33, 35, 37, 56, 96, 100, 128, 131, 152, 153, 155, 160, 163, 164	Pages: 78, 79
To use the present and past tenses correctly and consistently including the progressive form.	Pages: 10–11, 12–13	Pages: 58, 59, 63, 89	Pages: 16, 17, 18, 19, 20, 22, 23, 24, 80, 81, 82, 83, 84, 85
To use subordination (using 'when', 'if', 'that' or 'because') and co-ordination (using 'or', 'and' or 'but').	Pages: 16–17	Pages: 85, 90, 91, 93, 94, 95, 101, 148, 149, 155, 158, 163, 164, 184, 195, 197	Pages: 74, 75, 76, 77
To use some features of written Standard English.	Pages: 18–19	Pages: 96, 97, 119, 120, 123, 154, 155, 195	Pages: 84
To use and understand the grammatical terminology in Appendix 2 in discussing their writing: noun, noun phrase, statement, question, exclamation, command, compound, adjective, verb, suffix, adverb, tense (past, present), apostrophe, comma.	Pages: 6–7, 8	Pages: 23, 25, 26, 27, 55, 56, 58, 59, 60, 69, 83, 90, 93, 116, 196	Pages: 78, 79, 100–101
To form nouns using suffixes such as 'ness', 'er' and by compounding. (Grammar appendix)	Pages: 28–29, 49	Pages: 90, 96, 101, 125, 133, 195	Pages: 36, 37, 38, 39, 59, 60, 61, 62, 63–64, 65, 66
To form adjectives using suffixes such as 'ful', 'less'. (Grammar appendix)	Pages: 28–29	Pages: 90, 96, 101, 125, 133, 195	Pages: 36, 37, 38, 39, 59, 61, 62, 63–64
To use the suffixes 'er', 'est' in adjectives and 'ly' in Standard English to turn adjectives into adverbs. (Grammar appendix)	Pages: 14–15, 30–31	Pages: 13, 127, 151	Pages: 19, 20, 21, 22, 23, 24, 36, 38, 39, 59, 63, 64
To make the correct choice and consistent use of present tense and past tense throughout writing. (Grammar appendix)	Pages: 10–11	Pages: 57–59, 63–65, 83–85, 89–91, 119	Pages: 16, 17, 18, 19, 20, 80, 81, 82, 83
To use the progressive form of verbs in the present and past tense to mark actions in progress. (Grammar appendix)	Pages: 12–13	Pages: 57–59, 63–65, 83–85, 89–91, 101–103, 118–120, 194–196	Pages: 19, 20, 22, 23, 24, 84, 85
To use capital letters, full stops, question marks and exclamation marks to demarcate sentences. (Grammar appendix)	Pages: 20–21	Pages: 23, 25–27, 28–30, 60–62, 69, 92–94, 116, 133, 165	Pages: 67, 68, 69, 70, 71, 72, 73, 86, 87, 88
To use commas to separate items in a list. (Grammar appendix)	Pages: 22–23	Pages: 13, 27	Pages: 90, 91, 92, 93

Nouns and Nouns with capital letters

Prior learning

- Know that a noun names a person, place, thing or idea (happiness).
- Know that names of people and places, days of the week and the personal pronoun 'I' start with a capital letter.

Learn

- Write these words on the board: 'cat', 'horse', 'tree', 'school', 'hopping', 'yellow', 'teacher'.
- Remind the children that a noun names a person, place, thing or idea.
- Ask them to decide which of the words on the board are nouns. Talk about how the words 'hopping' and 'yellow' do not name a person, place, thing or idea, so they can't be nouns.
- Children use sticky notes to label nouns around the classroom.

- Challenge the children to think of nouns that they can't touch, such as the sky. Display a list of these abstract nouns.
- Use the shopping trip activity from *100 English Lessons Year 2, Autumn 1, Week 3, Lesson 4* to help the children identify that brand names have capital letters. Explain that nouns that name specific things (proper nouns) have capital letters. Use packaging to identify proper nouns.

- Ensure that children understand that the names of people and places have capital letters. Use environmental print to help them identify proper nouns.
- Point out that days of the week have capital letters and help the children to write and spell them. Do the same for the months of the year and specific holidays, such as Easter and Christmas.

Curriculum objectives

- To use and understand the term 'noun'. (Grammar appendix)

Success criteria

- I can recognise a noun.
- I know why some nouns start with capital letters.

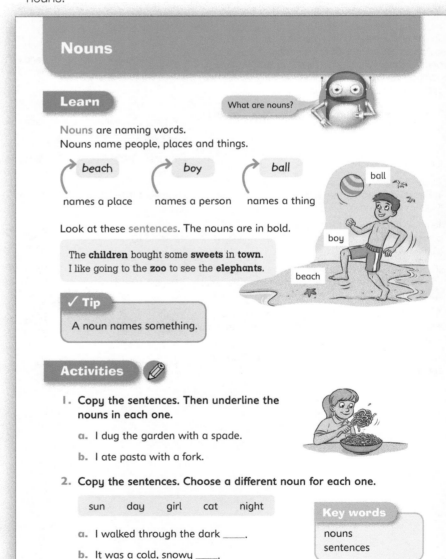

Nouns

Learn

What are nouns?

Nouns are naming words.
Nouns name people, places and things.

beach → names a place

boy → names a person

ball → names a thing

ball
boy
beach

Look at these sentences. The nouns are in bold.

The **children** bought some **sweets** in **town**.
I like going to the **zoo** to see the **elephants**.

✓ Tip

A noun names something.

Activities

1. **Copy the sentences. Then underline the nouns in each one.**

   a. I dug the garden with a spade.

   b. I ate pasta with a fork.

2. **Copy the sentences. Choose a different noun for each one.**

   | sun | day | girl | cat | night |

   Key words

   nouns
   sentences

   a. I walked through the dark _____.

   b. It was a cold, snowy _____.

- The textbook activities cover identifying common and proper nouns. Children are encouraged to choose the correct noun to complete a sentence. The links in *100 English Lessons Year 2* explore and reinforce the term 'noun'.

Write

- Write 'whale road' on the board. Tell the children that this a kenning, used by the Vikings to describe the sea. The kenning is made up of two nouns. (See pages 78-79 for more comprehensive information about kennings.)
- Write 'story weaver' on the board and ask the children who that could refer to (a writer or storyteller).

- Choose some everyday objects or people (teacher, smartphone, book, classroom) and ask the children if they can think of a suitable kenning.
- Ask the children to think of some nouns and write them on the board. Can any of these nouns be combined to make a kenning?
- Ask the children to choose their favourite kenning so far, or to create a new one and illustrate it so the reader knows what it describes.

Nouns with capital letters

Learn

Can nouns start with capital letters?

Some nouns start with capital letters.

These nouns name a particular person, place, day of the week or month of the year.

Names of people	Names of places
Josh	Blackpool
Irena	England
Mrs Brown	Africa

Names of days	Names of months
Monday	January
Saturday	March
Wednesday	November

GO Shopping Saturday

MARCH

Activities

1. **Copy the sentences. Then underline the nouns that start with a capital letter.**

   a. We gave our homework to Mr Patel.

   b. Our class go swimming every Tuesday.

2. **Copy the sentences. Then underline the nouns that should start with a capital letter.**

   a. I am going to menorca for my holiday.

   b. My birthday is in february.

   c. preston is on the river ribble.

> ✓ **Tip**
>
> If a noun is the name of a person, place, day or month, it starts with a capital letter.

Key words

capital letters

100 English Lessons Year 2 links:

- Starter activity 16 (page 15): Knowing terminology: 'noun'
- Autumn 1, Week 3 (pages 25–27): recognise nouns

Year 2 Practice Book links:

- (page 78): More information

Adjectives

Prior learning

- Know that a noun names a person, place, thing or idea (happiness).
- Understand that an adjective modifies a noun.

Learn

- Remind the children that nouns name a person, place, thing or idea. Ask them to tell you some nouns.
- Explain that words that give us more information about nouns are called adjectives.
- Ask the children to think of adjectives to describe the sizes of a mouse and a castle. Write these adjectives on the board.
- Adjectives can also tell us what the noun looks like. Ask the children to think of adjectives to describe what the mouse and the castle look like. Write these adjectives on the board.
- Photocopiable page 43 in *100 English Lessons Year 2* 'Tangy tomatoes' encourages children to use their senses to create adjectives to describe food.

Talk

- Display pictures of three everyday objects that look very different (such as three different teddy bears). The children choose one of the objects and describe it to their partner using adjectives. Can their partner work out which one they are describing?

Activities

- The textbook activity supports using adjectives to create accurate descriptions of nouns.

Curriculum objectives

- To use and understand the term 'adjective'. (Grammar appendix)

Success criteria

- I understand that adjectives give more information about nouns.

100 English Lessons Year 2 links:

- Starter activity 16 (page 15): knowing terminology: 'noun' and 'adjective'
- Autumn 1, Week 3 (pages 25–7): use adjectives

Year 2 Practice Book links:

- (pages 100–101): Finding out from charts
- (page 78): More information
- (page 79): What are they like?

Adjectives

Learn

Adjectives are describing words. They describe what a noun is like.

What are adjectives?

Here is a noun: house. What is the house like?

| a new house | a large house | a spooky house |

These three adjectives describe very different houses!

Activities

1. **Copy the sentences. Then underline the adjectives in each one.**

   a. They had a short walk home.

   b. A gigantic parcel arrived this morning.

2. **Copy the sentences. Write an adjective to complete each one.**

   a. At last they found the ____ treasure chest.

   b. We couldn't wait to arrive at the ____ castle.

> ✓ **Tip**
>
> Try using these adjectives in sentences to make your writing more interesting.
>
> **enormous   magnificent   gloomy
> delicious   exciting   comfortable**

Key words

adjectives

Noun phrases

Prior learning

- Know that a noun names a person, place, thing or idea.
- Understand that an adjective modifies a noun.

Learn

- Write 'the hat' on the board. Ask the children what sort of word 'hat' is. Explain that a noun names a person, place, thing or idea. Ask the children to imagine the hat. Take feedback.

- Explain that you can visualise the hat better by adding some information with a noun phrase.
- Write 'the black hat'. Explain that 'black' is an adjective and describes the hat. What does the hat look like now?
- Over several sessions, introduce using more than one adjective in a noun phrase. Discuss how this further clarifies the noun.

Activities

- The textbook activity covers identifying and creating noun phrases using adjectives. Noun phrases used to describe and specify appear throughout the *100 English Lessons Year 2*.

Curriculum objectives

- To use expanded noun phrases to describe and specify.

Success criteria

- I can give more information about a noun by writing a noun phrase.

100 English Lessons Year 2 links:

- Starter activity (page 11): 'Why say one word'
- Autumn 1, Week 3 (pages 25–27): use noun phrases to add information
- Autumn 1, Assess and review (pages 37–39): use noun phrases to specify independently
- Autumn 2, Week 2 (pages 54–56): describe a setting using noun phrases
- Spring 2, Week 5 (page 128): Lesson 3, Using the senses
- Summer 1, Week 3 (pages 153–155): create noun phrases using adjectives
- Summer 2, Week 6 (pages 194–196): extend sentences using expanded noun phrases

Year 2 Practice Book links:

- (page 78): More information
- (page 79): What are they like?

Noun phrases

Learn

What are noun phrases?

Noun phrases are groups of words that include a noun.

A noun phrase can be made up of an adjective and a noun.

adjective + noun = noun phrase

✓ Tip

You can use more than one adjective to make your noun phrases even better!

the cute, tabby kitten

a windy day

adjective + noun = noun phrase

the kind teacher

adjective + noun = noun phrase

Activities

Key words

noun phrases

1. **Copy the sentences. Then underline the noun phrase in each one.**

   a. It was an interesting book.

   b. The train took us on a long, boring journey.

2. **Write a noun phrase to match each picture.**

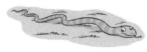

a ____, ____ lion   the ____, ____ snake

Grammatical words   **9**

Verbs: present tense and Verbs: past tense

Prior learning

- Know that verbs are doing and being words.
- Know that we need verbs to create clauses and sentences.

Learn

- The focus of this section is to identify the simple past and present tense. Children will use this understanding to write sentences in the simple past or present tense in stories and recounts.
- Ensure the children understand the concept of the past by getting them to talk about events that have happened to them. Help them to use the simple present tense by narrating an event as it happens, such as 'Lucy walks in the door. She sits at her desk. She takes out her book. She reads her book.' (Try not to use the progressive tense.)
- The interactive activity on the *100 English Lessons Year 2* CD-ROM 'In the past' provides practice writing the past tense.
- Many verbs are irregular in the past tense and some of these are identified in the textbook activity. Extend this list by asking confident learners to look out for irregular past-tense verbs in their reading.
- Write a simple sentence such as 'I ride my bike'. Help children identify how the present tense changes (adding an 's') for he/she/it.

Curriculum objectives

- To use the present and past tenses correctly and consistently including the progressive form.
- To make the correct choice and consistent use of present tense and past tense throughout writing. (Grammar appendix)

Success criteria

- I know that verbs are doing and being words.
- I know that the present tense describes actions that are happening now.
- I know that the past tense describes actions that have happened.
- I can identify and write verbs in the present and past tense.

Verbs: present tense

Learn

What are verbs and what is the present tense?

Most **verbs** are doing words. They tell us what someone or something *does*.

Some verbs are being words. They tell us what someone or something *is*.

Verbs in the **present tense** describe actions that are happening now.

These verbs all describe what someone is doing now.

he **sleeps**

she **writes**

they **walk**

These verbs are all being words.

I am	he is	you are

They are all written in the present tense.

Key words

verbs
present tense

Activities

1. **Copy these sentences. Then underline the verbs in each one.**

   a. Jack draws a picture of a train.

   b. They eat their sandwiches hungrily.

2. **Write each sentence in the present tense.**

   a. We looked in the shops for a football.

   b. She watched a very scary film.

✓ Tip

Does the word tell us what someone or something is doing?

If it does, it's a verb!

- Ensure the children understand how to conjugate the verbs 'to be', 'to do' and 'to have' in the present tense. Help them spot these verbs in the contracted forms such as 'I'm', 'he's', 'we've', and so on.
- The *100 English Lessons Year 2* contains many activities that embed the use of past and present tense verbs in writing.

Activities

- The textbook activities concentrate on explaining the simple past and present tenses, ensuring that children can both identify and write these tenses.
- Use the matching activity in *100 English Lessons Year 2* (page 77) 'Past and present' to reinforce understanding of the simple past and present tense.

- The grammar activities in the *Year 2 Practice Book* reinforce the simple past and present tense and can be used to support children who need more practice.
- The suffix 'ed' creates the past tense for many verbs. This does have implications for spelling. Remind children of the swap, double or drop rules for adding suffixes and use the spelling activities in the *Year 2 Practice Book* to reinforce them.

Verbs: past tense

Learn

What is the past tense?

Verbs in the past tense describe actions that have already happened.

Add **ed** to make the past tense of most verbs.

Present tense	Past tense
she cooks	she cooked
I watch	I watched
we paint	we painted

Some verbs form their past tense differently. You do not add **ed**.

Present tense	Past tense
I drink	I drank
he sleeps	he slept
you buy	you bought

Key words

past tense

Activities

1. Copy the table and include the verbs that are missing.

Present tense	Past tense
we clean	we
I	I helped
he talks	he
they	they pushed

✓ **Tip**

Watch out! Not all verbs form the past tense by adding **ed**.

2. Copy the sentences. Write each verb in the past tense.

a. **pull** We ____ the rope on to the boat.

b. **eat** She ____ her meal slowly.

Grammatical words 11

100 English Lessons Year 2 links:

- Autumn 2, Week 3 (pages 57–59): write accurate sentences in the past tense
- Autumn 2, Week 5 (pages 63–65): use the past tense consistently in a diary entry
- Spring 1, Week 1 (pages 83–85): identify past or present tense verbs
- Spring 1, Week 3 (pages 89–91): use the past tense correctly and consistently in a recount
- Spring 2, Week 2 (page 119) Lesson 2, Using Standard English

Year 2 Practice Book links:

- (pages 16–20): Swap and drop rules when adding 's' and 'ed'
- (page 80): In the past
- (page 81): Matching past and present
- (page 82): Spot the s!
- (page 83): Hare and Tortoise

Verbs: present tenses with 'ing' and Verbs: past tenses with 'ing'

Prior learning

- Know that the present tense describes actions that are happening now.
- Know that the past tense describes actions that have happened.
- Can identify and write verbs in the simple present and past tense.
- Know the verb 'to be' in the past and present tense.

Learn

- The focus of this section is to identify the progressive past and progressive present tense and use this understanding in stories, a diary entry and a recount.
- Ensure children understand the concept of the past by getting them to talk about events that have happened to them. Help them to use the progressive

tense by talking about events that happen over a period of time, such as 'Last night I was reading my book when the cat walked in.' or 'Jim is writing a fantastic story.' Ask the children to identify which tense your sentences are in.

- Write the past and present tense of the verb 'to be' ('I am', 'he is', 'they are') to ensure that children know how to conjugate it.
- Make sure the children understand that the progressive

tense is made up of an auxiliary verb (helper verb) 'is'/'are'/'am' or 'was'/'were' and the main verb ending in 'ing'. Explain that it is the tense of the helper verb that makes the past or the present tense in progressive verbs.

- Help the children identify the progressive tense in a range of stories and recount writing as suggested in *100 English Lessons Year 2*.

Curriculum objectives

- To use the present and past tenses correctly and consistently including the progressive form.
- To use the progressive form of verbs in the present and past tense to mark actions in progress. (Grammar appendix)

Success criteria

- I know that verbs ending in 'ing' describe actions that are still happening.
- I can use 'am'/'is' added to a verb ending in 'ing' to describe an action happening in the present.
- I can use 'was'/'were' added to a verb ending in 'ing' to describe an action that started happening in the past.

Verbs: present tenses with 'ing'

Learn

What are present tenses with **ing**?

Sometimes we need to describe actions that are still happening now, or that were happening in the past. To do this we use a being verb with a doing verb ending in **ing**.

We can describe actions in the **present** that **are** happening now. To do this we use the being verbs am, is or are + the doing verb ending ing.

am		I am jumping
is	+ doing verb and ing	he is jumping
are		they are jumping

Activities

1. **Copy these sentences. Choose the correct verb from: 'is', 'am' and 'are'.**
   a. Ellie _____ washing her hair tonight.
   b. Auntie Kath and Uncle Richard _____ taking me to the cinema.
   c. I _____ eating my tea.

   > ✓ **Tip**
   > am, is and are are sometimes called helper verbs.

2. **Write the words that show the actions which are happening now.**
   a. I am walking with my gran and grandad.
   b. The trees are blowing in the wind.

3. **Use the helper verbs to rewrite these sentences so they describe something which is happening now.**
   a. We go to the pool.
   b. I swim backstroke.

Activities

- The textbook clearly explains how past and present progressive tenses are formed. Children identify and write verbs in both tenses.

- Children can use the grammar activities in the *Year 2 Practice Book* to write the present progressive tense and identify the past progressive tense. Remind them that it's all about the helper verbs!

- The activities in *100 English Lessons Year 2* embed use of the progressive tense within writing. It would be helpful to model writing sentences such as 'The giraffes were eating calmly when the escaped lion prowled by.' Children can see that both verbs are in the past tense and retain tense consistency.

100 English Lessons Year 2 links:

- Autumn 2, Week 3 (pages 57–59): use the past progressive tense correctly in a story

- Autumn 2, Week 5 (pages 63–65): know when to use the present progressive and past tense

- Spring 1, Week 1 (pages 83–85): use the past, present and progressive tenses correctly

- Spring 1, Week 3 (pages 89–91): use the simple and progressive past tense to describe action in a recount

- Spring 1, Assess and review (pages 101–103): use the simple and progressive past tense to describe action in an independently written story

- Spring 2, Week 2 (pages 118–120): identify verb-tense cohesion in a story

- Summer 2, Week 6 (pages 194–196): write a story ensuring tense cohesion

Year 2 Practice Book links:

- (pages 19): Lose the 'e'
- (pages 20): Root words
- (page 22): What are they doing?
- (pages 23–24): Doubling up and Double trouble
- (page 84): What are they doing today?
- (page 85): Back in time

Verbs: past tenses with 'ing'

Learn

*How do we use past tenses with **ing**?*

We can describe actions in the **past** that **were** happening.

To do this, we use the being verbs was and were + the doing verb ending ing.

| was
was   + doing verb and ing
were | I **was** reading
he **was** reading
they **were** reading | [Insert a/w of children reading a book/Kindle] |

Activities

1. **These events have already happened. Write the sentences. Add the correct verbs to complete them.**

   a. The children were _____ sandcastles.

   b. Jane was _____ her bike.

   c. I was _____ television.

> **Use the helper verbs: was, were.**

2. **Use the helper verbs to write a sentence about each picture to show what each person was doing yesterday.**

a.
b.
c.
d.
e.
f.

> ✓ **Tip**
>
> **was** and **were** are sometimes called helper verbs.

Grammatical words   13

Adverbs

Prior learning

- Know that verbs are doing and being words.
- Know that a noun names a person, place, thing or idea.
- Understand that an adjective modifies a noun.

Learn

- Ensure that the children can identify verbs in sentences.
- Write the sentence 'Jake eats cake.' Ask the children to identify the verb. Say you want to tell the reader how Jake ate the cake. Change the sentence to 'Jake eats cake greedily.' Explain that 'greedily' helps the reader understand exactly how Jake eats the cake. Ask the children to think of other words to describe how Jake eats the cake. Use their words in the sentence. Explain that these words are called adverbs and they give us more information about how the verb is being carried out.

- Introduce the children to other sentences with adverbs that show how a verb is being carried out. Note that not all adverbs end in the suffix 'ly'. Practise using the adverbs in different places in the sentence, as shown in the textbook.
- Choose adjectives to change into adverbs such as 'happy', 'sad', 'grumpy', 'beautiful' and 'angry'.

Write these on the board. Ensure that the children understand that these words can be used to give more information about nouns. Add the suffix 'ly' to the adjectives and challenge the children to use them as adverbs.
- Draw the children's attention to how a root word changes (or not) when the suffix 'ly' is added.

Curriculum objectives

- To use the suffixes 'er' and 'est' in adjectives and to use 'ly' in Standard English to turn adjectives into adverbs. (Grammar appendix)

Success criteria

- I know that adverbs give me more information about verbs.
- I can recognise an adverb.
- I can add the suffix 'ly' to an adjective to make an adverb.
- I can choose the right adverb to complete a sentence.

Adverbs

Learn

What are adverbs?

Adverbs describe verbs. They describe how something is done.

He runs quickly.
→ verb   ↑ adverb

The adverb describes **how** he runs.

Carefully, she walked on the ice.
↖ adverb   ↑ verb

The adverb describes **how** she walked on the ice.

Adverbs often end with **ly**.

| slowly | softly | stupidly | roughly |

clumsy → clumsily
cheeky → cheekily

Key words

adverbs

✓ **Tip**

To make an adverb from a word ending in y, change y to i and add **ly**.

14   Grammatical words

- The textbook clearly explains what adverbs are and how they can be formed from adjectives. Children identify and write adverbs.

- Support children by writing a simple sentence such as 'Raina runs home.' Play about with the sentence, using different adverbs to describe how Raina runs and ask the children to help you. Encourage them to write a sentence using an adverb.

Make sure they have lots of oral rehearsal before they write.

- Use the spelling activities in the *Year 2 Practice Book* to focus on when to swap, double or drop when adding the suffix 'ly'. Use the vocabulary activity 'What kind of action?' (pages 63–64) to practise identifying adverbs.

- When you model writing in the *100 English Lessons Year 2* writing lessons, use adverbs sparingly. It is often better to use a more accurate verb rather than an adverb.

Activities

1. **Write these adjectives as adverbs.**
   For example: bright *brightly*

   a. quiet

   b. greedy

   c. happy

   d. heavy

   > ✓ **Tip**
   >
   > Adverbs make your sentences exciting! Can you think of more adverbs to use in your sentences?

2. **Copy the sentences. Then underline the adverbs.**

   a. I walked slowly to school in the rain.

   b. My friend was happily talking to her mum.

   c. The snow fell silently on to the garden.

3. **Copy this sentence. Choose an adverb to complete it.**

   | noisily | silently | up |

   The birds sang _____ as the sun rose in the sky.

4. **Rewrite this sentence and change the adverb.**
   The children laughed loudly at the clown's silliness.

Grammatical words   15

100 English Lessons Year 2 links:

- Starter activity 10 (page 13): Add a suffix

- Started activity 16 (page 15): Knowing terminology

Year 2 Practice Book links:

- (page 20): Root words

- (page 21): Drop the 'y', add the 'i'

- (page 36): Suffixes

- (page 38): How does it end?

- (page 39): It all adds up

- (pages 63–64): What kind of action?

Joining words and More joining words

Prior learning

- Know what a sentence is.
- Can join words and sentences using 'and'.

Learn

- One way to add information to a sentence is to use a joining word such as 'or', 'and' or 'but'. Show the children how these conjunctions can join words, phrases and main clauses. Start off with co-ordinating conjunctions such as *'Do you want chips or mash?'* or *'I like tea and cake.'* Expand the sentences to include noun phrases. Finally, show the children how 'or', 'and' or 'but' join main clauses together.
- Use 'Joining Words' and 'School day' in the *Year 2 Practice Book* to reinforce the use of co-ordinating conjunctions.
- Show the children how the subordinating conjunctions 'when', 'if', 'that' or 'because' can be used to add further

information to a main clause. Discuss how these words join different types of information to the main clause: 'when' will typically add information about time or cause, 'because' often gives more information why.
- Identify how 'when', 'if', 'that' or 'because' are used in the stories, picture books and other texts in *100 English Lessons Year 2*. Challenge children to find other examples in their reading.

- Subordinating conjunctions join a main clause to a subordinate clause. They typically add information to a main clause and can start a sentence, unlike a co-ordinating conjunction. Children in Year 2 do not need to know about these technical details or language yet, but it is important that you are aware so you don't cause confusion later on.

Curriculum objectives

- To use subordination ('when', 'if', 'that' or 'because') and co–ordination ('or', 'and' or 'but').

Success criteria

- I can identify the joining words 'or', 'and', 'but', 'when', 'if', 'that' or 'because' in a sentence.
- I can join words, groups of words and sentences using 'or', 'and' or 'but'.
- I can add extra information to a sentence using 'when', 'if', 'that' or 'because'.

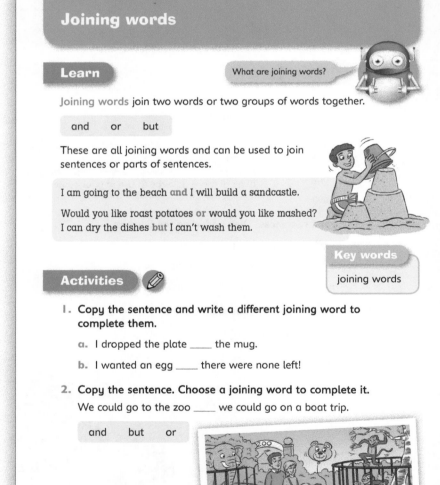

Joining words

Learn

What are joining words?

Joining words join two words or two groups of words together.

| and | or | but |

These are all joining words and can be used to join sentences or parts of sentences.

I am going to the beach **and** I will build a sandcastle.

Would you like roast potatoes **or** would you like mashed?
I can dry the dishes **but** I can't wash them.

Key words

joining words

Activities

1. Copy the sentence and write a different joining word to complete them.

    a. I dropped the plate _____ the mug.

    b. I wanted an egg _____ there were none left!

2. Copy the sentence. Choose a joining word to complete it.

    We could go to the zoo _____ we could go on a boat trip.

    | and | but | or |

16 Grammatical words

- Model using 'or', 'and' or 'but', 'when', 'if', 'that' or 'because' in shared writing. Talk about the job these joining words do when they join clauses. Give children opportunities to practise using these joining words in short, fun writing tasks.

- To support less confident learners, use the photocopiable sheet on the *100 English Lessons*

Year 2 CD-ROM 'Subordination and coordination', which allows them to match the beginning clause of a sentence with a subordinating or co-ordinating clause.

Activities

- The activities in the textbook explain joining words and help children practise using them in sentences.

- The activities in *100 English Lessons Year 2* embed use of these conjunctions within the writing process.

100 English Lessons Year 2 links:

- Spring 1, Weeks 1–5 (pages 83–97): add additional information to a sentence using the conjunctions 'and', 'when','if', 'that' and 'because'

- Spring 1, Assess and review (page 101): Practising subordination and coordination

- Summer 1, Weeks 1–3 (pages 147–155): use co-ordinating and subordinating conjunctions to organise and extend sentences

- Summer 1, Week 6 (pages 162–164): evaluate the impact of subordinate clauses in children's writing

- Summer 2, Week 2 (pages 182–184): use conjunctions in a ship's log

- Summer 2, Week 6 (pages 194–196): draft writing to improve use of subordinating and co-ordinating conjunctions

- Summer 2, Assess and review (pages 197–199): extend sentences using co-ordination and subordination

Year 2 Practice Book links:

- (page 74): Joining words
- (page 75): School day
- (page 76): More joining words
- (page 77): The ball

More joining words

Learn

What else do joining words do?

Some joining words join extra information to a sentence.

| when | because | if | that |

The end of the sentence gives extra information about the first part.

Joe walks the dog **when** he gets home from school.
Let me know **if** you would like a drink.
We went to a forest **that** has an adventure trail.
I didn't finish my homework **because** the baby was crying.

A joining word does not have to be in the middle of a sentence.

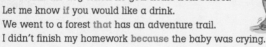

When it is my birthday, I will see my gran.

Activities

1. **Copy the sentences. Then underline the joining word in each one.**

   a. It was after dark when the owl began to hoot.

   b. If the car needs petrol, we will need to stop.

2. **Rewrite the sentences. Choose the <u>same</u> joining word to complete them.**

   _____ I am eight years old, I will go into the next swimming group.

   They would have their tea _____ it was ready.

Standard English

Prior learning

- Can recognise a sentence.
- Understand that writing follows rules.
- Can recognise verbs.
- Understand past and present tenses.

Learn

- Explain that everybody has their own special way of talking, and that in different areas of the country (and the world) English is spoken in different ways. There are local words to describe things like food, places and people. People might have special phrases to describe what they do and where they go. When we write, we have to use a type of English that everyone understands, no matter where they come from. This is called Standard English.
- Ensure the children understand how to conjugate the verb 'to be' and 'to have' in both the past and present tenses: see the previous activities on formation of the past, present and progressive tenses for further support.
- Show the children how the verb form changes depending on who is carrying out the verb. Swap the pronouns for people, for instance 'she is' = 'Jane is', 'they are' = 'Joe and Sharif are'.
- **Note** that subject-verb agreement can be particularly confusing for young children when they use the progressive tense.

- Help children think about how they can write concisely when planning. Show them how Standard English helps to get rid of extra words. In this way, they can concentrate on their message/the information they want to convey.

Curriculum objectives

- To use some features of written Standard English.

Success criteria

- I can write using sentences.
- I can make the verbs in my sentences match the number of people.
- I can write information clearly so that everyone can understand it.

Standard English

Learn

What is Standard English?

Standard English is English with correct grammar, punctuation and spelling.

Verbs should match the number of objects or people.

Wrong ✗	Right ✔
I is	I am
he were	he was
they was	they were

Key words

Standard English

No slang!
It was right hot! → It was very hot!
Go and pick them apples. → Go and pick those apples.

Check what you mean:
I could of scored a goal. → I could have scored a goal.
They should of won the race. → They should have won the race.

Say 'no' once:
I didn't eat no sweets. → I didn't eat any sweets.
He couldn't remember nothing. → He couldn't remember anything.

- Help children understand the different voices we use when writing and speaking. Pretend that Queen Elizabeth is coming to school.

- Ask the children to think about how they would talk to her. How would they ensure that she understood everything they said?

- Together, draw up a list of common slang/non-Standard English. Translate these phrases into Standard English.

Activities

- Following Lesson 2 in *100 English Lessons Year 2* (page 119) 'Using Standard English', write non-Standard English sentences on the board and get the children to help you correct them. This will help them identify mistakes they may be making in their writing.

- Use the activities in the textbook incrementally to focus on different aspects of non-Standard English such as slang, double negatives and subject-verb agreement. Find examples of these non-Standard forms and work together to see how inaccurate they are and how they could lead to confusion for the reader. Ensure children understand that Standard English is needed to make our writing clear. It is especially important when they are writing information texts that have a wide audience. Throughout these activities, make sure that children understand that their dialect, accent and non-standard ways of speaking are all valid and valued.

Activities

1. **Rewrite these sentences so that they are in Standard English.**
   a. I goes to school every day.
   b. They is helping me to do my homework.
   c. The cat were drinking her milk greedily.

2. a. List the words in this sentence that are not in Standard English.
      He would of loved to go on the trip but it was right dear.
   b. Rewrite the above sentence in Standard English.

3. **Choose one part of each carriage to help you write a sentence in Standard English.**

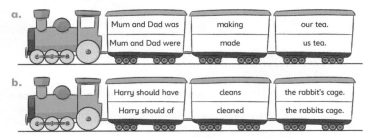

a.
| Mum and Dad was | making | our tea. |
| Mum and Dad were | made | us tea. |

b.
| Harry should have | cleans | the rabbit's cage. |
| Harry should of | cleaned | the rabbits cage. |

4. **Listen to your friends talking. Write down three sentences or phrases which are not in Standard English. Then change them into Standard English.**

> ✓ **Tip**
>
> You don't need to use Standard English for talking to friends and family, but it is better to use Standard English for writing and for talking to important people.

100 English Lessons Year 2 links:

- Spring 1, Week 5 (page 96): Lesson 2, Zoo maps

- Spring 2, Week 2 (pages 118–120): understand how spoken English may not follow the same rules as Standard English

- Spring 2, Week 3 (page 123): Lesson 5, Writing a report

- Summer 1, Week 3 (page 154): Lesson 3, Our nature walk

- Summer 2, Week 6 (page 195): Lesson 3, Extending sentences

Year 2 Practice Book links:

- (page 84): What are they doing today?

Sentence types

Prior learning

- Know that a sentence requires a verb.
- Know the punctuation used to demarcate a sentence.

- Review what a sentence is and the punctuation used to demarcate one sentence from another. Ensure children understand that it needs a verb.
- Identify statements, questions, exclamations and commands within texts. Help children to understand how each sentence type is formed and punctuated.

Curriculum objectives

- To learn how to use both familiar and new punctuation correctly, including full stops, capital letters, exclamation marks, question marks.
- To write sentences with different forms: statement, question, exclamation, command.
- To use capital letters, full stops, question marks and exclamation marks to demarcate sentences. (Grammar appendix)

Success criteria

- I can identify sentences that are statements, questions, exclamations and commands.
- I can write statements, questions, exclamations and commands.
- I know that a question requires a question mark.
- I know that exclamation marks can be used to show feelings and to make a command more forceful.

- Collect words that start and end questions. Include words and phrases such as 'when', 'where', 'how', 'can', 'isn't it' and 'does'. Help children identify questions by looking at the punctuation.
- Explore how exclamation marks are used to give feeling to sentences as well as to mark exclamations. Help children understand that some exclamations start with 'what' and 'how' and must include a verb.

- Statements are all sentences that give information, description or give opinions. Generally they end with full stops, but they can end with exclamation marks.

Talk

- Encourage children to ask and answer questions as part of the reading process.
- Play games such as 'Simon says' and 'Captain's orders' to establish that commands start

---

Sentence types: statements and questions

Learn

What are the different sentence types?

There are four types of sentence: statements, questions, exclamations and commands.

All sentences start with a capital letter.

A **statement** states a fact. It ends with a **full stop**.

Key words

statement
question

 It is a red car. I like ice cream.

A **question** asks a question. It ends with a **question mark**.

 What time is it? When will it be sunny?

Activities

1. **Write these sentence and decide if it is a statement or a question.**

   a. Why did you go to the shops?

   b. It is a new house.

   c. The dog is very muddy.

   d. Who wants a drink?

   ✓ **Tip**

   Questions often start with **When, What, Which, Who, Why** and **How**.

with imperative verbs. Help children understand how to give clear instructions/commands by playing games where one child instructs another. Allow them time to refine their commands.

Activities

- Use the interactive activity and photocopiable sheet 'Fairy-tale punctuation' and photocopiable page 108 'Sorting and punctuating sentences' from

100 English Lessons Year 2 to reinforce children's understanding of the four functions of sentences.

- The textbook explains the different sentence types. There are exercises to identify all four functions.
- Use the numerous activities in the *Year 2 Practice Book* to identify the different sentence types, choose the correct punctuation and write statements, questions, exclamations and commands.

100 English Lessons Year 2 links:

- Autumn 1, Week 2 (page 23): Lesson 3, Who will help me?
- Autumn 1, Week 3 (pages 25–27): identify imperative verbs in commands
- Autumn 1, Week 4 (pages 28–30): use imperative verbs to write commands
- Autumn 2, Week 4 (pages 60–62): write instructions for a board game using commands
- Autumn 2, Assess and review (page 69): Punctuating different sentence types
- Spring 1, Week 4 (pages 92–94): punctuate statements, questions, exclamations and commands
- Spring 2, Week 1 (page 116): Lesson 2, Sentence types
- Spring 2, Assess and review (page 133): Writing questions
- Summer 1, Assess and review (page 165): Writing different types of sentences

Year 2 Practice Book links:

- (page 67): Tell me
- (page 68): What happened here?
- (page 69): Question mark challenge
- (page 70): Guess the questions
- (page 71): How does it end?
- (page 72): What are they saying?
- (page 73): Jack's hat
- (page 86): The fox and the crow
- (page 87): Andrew's muddy day
- (page 88): Talking to the giant

Sentence types: exclamations and commands

Learn

An **exclamation** shows excitement, surprise or emotion.

It ends with an exclamation **mark**.

Key words

exclamation
command

| How fantastic your hair looks! | What a scary film we watched! |

A **command** tells someone to do something.

It can end with an **exclamation mark** or a **full stop**.

Tidy up! ← Forceful command. Ends with an exclamation mark.

Tidy up, please. ← Not as forceful. Ends with a full stop.

Activities

1. **Copy these sentences and decide what type each one is. Write the type next to each one.**

   | statement | question | exclamation | command |

   a. Go home

   b. How much has it grown

   c. How clever you are

   d. It was planted last week

2. **Add a question mark, a full stop or an exclamation mark to complete each sentence from activity 1.**

Punctuation **21**

Commas in lists

Prior learning

- Know why we might need lists.
- Can identify lists without commas.

Learn

- Establish when the children have used or seen lists in everyday life. Talk about how a list could be used in information writing and stories.

- Write a shopping list vertically on the board and model how you turn it into a list within a sentence starting 'I will need…'. Show how a comma separates each item. Explain how this helps the reader know exactly what they need. Model how 'and' is used to join the final item to the list. The 'and' replaces the comma and separates the final two items.

- Play games such as 'When granny went shopping' in *100 English Lessons Year 2* (page 27) 'Let's go shopping' to help children understand the purpose of commas in lists.

Curriculum objectives

- To learn how to use both familiar and new punctuation correctly, including commas for lists.
- To use commas to separate items in a list. (Grammar appendix)

Success criteria

- I can write commas to separate items in a list.

Commas in lists

Learn

How are commas used?

Commas are used to separate items in a list.

Use commas to separate a list of objects.

> We used a mango, strawberries, a lime and apples to make a smoothie.

Use a comma after each item. **Do not** use a comma before *and*.

> Josh, Anwar, Omar, Tomas and Oliver came to my party.

✓ Tip

You need a comma after each item in a list. Do not use a comma before *and*.

Key words

commas

Activities

1. **Copy these sentences and add commas to the correct places.**

   a. I have a sandwich yoghurt crisps and a drink in my lunch box.

   b. September April June and November all have thirty days.

   c. He washed all the mugs bowls plates and spoons.

   d. They did maths science art and PE on Monday.

- The textbook introduces how to use commas to separate items in lists. It also explains how to use 'and' to separate the final two items in a list.

- There are several activities that reinforce how to use commas in lists in the *Year 2 Practice Book*. These give ample punctuation practice.

- If children need additional support, use physical items to create lists. Make commas on card and ask the children to place the commas between each item. Model how to turn the physical list into a written list and then encourage children to write their own list.

- Following on from the textbook activities ask the children to write lists of the ingredients for a fairy tale. Explain that you need exact details in the list so you can write a fantastic story. Model expanding the nouns within your list into noun phrases, for example 'a prince' becomes 'a handsome prince'. Ensure you model how the comma separates each item. Ask the children to add detail to their nouns. Can they remember where the commas should go?

---

2. **Copy the sentence which uses commas correctly.**

   - The rescue centre helps dogs, cats, rabbits, and guinea pigs.
   - Girls, and boys both like playing football cricket and, netball.
   - My grandparents, cousins, aunts and uncles all came to my party.

3. **Use the lists below to finish these sentences. Use four items in each list.**

   Remember to use a comma to separate each item.

Toys	Flowers	Clothes	Colours
marbles	sunflowers	jumper	blue
dolls	daffodils	trousers	green
balls	roses	dress	yellow
cars	pansies	T-shirt	red
bricks	marigolds	socks	orange

   a. My favourite flowers are ____.

   b. The toys I like playing with are ____.

   c. When I get dressed I put on my ____.

   d. The colours ____ are all in a rainbow.

4. **Who are your friends? Write a sentence listing four of your friends.**

   My friends are ____.

5. **What are your favourite foods? Write a sentence listing your four favourite foods.**

   My favourite foods are ____.

6. **What are your favourite hobbies? Write a sentence listing four of your favourite hobbies.**

   My favourite hobbies are ____.

100 English Lessons Year 2 links:

- Starter activity 8 (page 13): Commas in lists
- Autumn 1, Week 3 (page 27): Lesson 4, Let's go shopping

Year 2 Practice Book links:

- (page 90): Take a break!
- (page 91): Packing list
- (page 92): What's on the bed?
- (page 93): Picnic time

Apostrophes to show missing letters

Prior learning

- Can conjugate the verbs 'to be' and 'to have'.
- Can use 'not' to make a negative.

Learn

- **Note** it is vital that children understand the full form of the words before they use an apostrophe to contract them; this is because the verb is often 'hidden' in contractions (I'm, I am, I've, I have). Ensure the children are clear about the verbs 'to be' and 'to have' before you teach them the contracted versions.

- Introduce contracted words gradually. Ensure that the children understand that the second word is contracted but its meaning is retained. Model which letters are being missed out and explain how the apostrophe stands in their stead. Teach children to reverse the process so that they can turn contracted words into their full versions.

- Make a display of the contracted and full-version words side by side. Add to it over time as children discover more words through their reading.

- Use the interactive activity on the *100 English Lessons Year 2* CD-ROM 'Can't, don't, won't' to practise making negative contractions. Draw attention to how 'won't' (will not) changes entirely in its contracted form.

Curriculum objectives

- To learn to spell more words with contracted forms.
- To learn how to use both familiar and new punctuation correctly, including apostrophes for contracted forms and the possessive (singular).

Success criteria

- I understand that an apostrophe can show where letters are missing in a contracted word.
- I can use an apostrophe to show where letters are missing.
- I can turn a contracted word back into its original form.

Apostrophes to show missing letters

Learn   How are apostrophes used?

An apostrophe can be used in place of missing letters.

When we join words together we use an apostrophe to show where letters have been missed out.

In these words, the apostrophe shows where the letter **o** has been missed out.

could not	did not	is not
↓	↓	↓
couldn't	didn't	isn't

Key words

apostrophe

We can also use an apostrophe to join these words:

I am = I'm	it is = it's	we are = we're
they have = they've	here is = here's	we will = we'll

There are lots of others!

Activities

1. **Rewrite the sentences. Join the words in bold using an apostrophe.**

   a. I **have not** finished my lunch.

   b. We **can not** reach it.

   c. The children **were not** enjoying the pantomime.

   d. **You will** have to pay for the tickets now.

- We often use contractions when speaking, and many children's books use contractions. Play 'The incredible expanding word game' to change the contraction back to the full form, such as 'We are going on a bear hunt!', so the children can see the effect of the contraction in writing.

- Note the progressive tense is often harder to find if the auxiliary verb 'to be' is in the contracted form (I'm, we're, they're, he's).

- The textbook explains how contracted words are formed and where to place the apostrophe. Children can practise how to make contracted words as well as how to revert contracted words to their original form.

- The activities in the *Year 2 Practice Book* challenge children to apply their knowledge.

- Collect contracted words from different types of text. Enjoy playing with some of the more playful contracted words such as the pirate language in *100 English Lessons Year 2* (page 181).

2. **Write these joined words in full.**

   a. I've

   b. doesn't

   c. they're

   d. what's

   e. wasn't

   f. could've

Can you work out the missing letters in these joined words?

3. **Write the two words which each word in bold stands for.**

   a. **It's** snowing now.

   b. **It'll** be a long journey tomorrow.

   c. **I'd** like a cake, please.

   d. **He'd** given them a present.

4. **Copy the words below and then write the joined word next to each one. For example:** she is = *she's*

   a. I am

   b. they were not

   c. we did not

   d. he would

   e. they have

5. **Choose a story book. How many joined words can you find? Write the words and work out what the full words would be.**

100 English Lessons Year 2 links:

- Autumn 1, Week 2 (page 23): Lesson 2, Contractions

- Autumn 1, Week 5 (page 32): Lesson 3, Planning a poster

- Autumn 1, Assess and review (page 37): Contractions

- Autumn 2, Assess and review (page 69): Consolidating contractions

- Spring 2, Week 4 (page 125): Lesson 2, Contractions

- Summer 2, Week 1 (page 181): Lesson 5, Contraction competition

- Summer 2, Week 6 (pages 194–196): identify contracted words

Year 2 Practice Book links:

- (page 40): Shorten it

- (page 41): Party on Mars

- (page 42): That's my home

- (page 43): What's the fairy tale?

- (page 94): It's in the tree

- (page 95): A snowy day

- (page 97): Pirate Black's map

Apostrophes to show belonging

Prior learning

- Terminology: noun, plural.
- Know how the apostrophe is used as a contraction.

Learn

- **Note** that after learning about the apostrophe for possession, many children get confused and use this apostrophe with plural words. The National Curriculum tries to circumvent this problem by introducing singular possession first. However, be on the alert for a rash of inaccurate punctuation! Teach the children to think 'Does the 's' mean more than one or belonging to?' In this way they are more likely to make the right choice (more often!).

- Write 'the hat belonging to Gran' on the board. Introduce possessive apostrophes by explaining that there is a quicker way to write this that uses the apostrophe and the letter 's'. Write 'Gran's hat' and explain how the apostrophe and the letter 's' are doing the job of the words 'belonging to'.

- Use the texts that you read in class to identify possessive apostrophes. Draw attention to how possessive apostrophes are used with names, especially those ending in 's'.

- Use the interactive activity on the *100 English Lessons Year 2* CD-ROM 'Possessive apostrophes' to understand and practise possessive apostrophes.

- Make sure that the children can distinguish between the job that apostrophe + 's' does and the job that 's' on its own does when it makes plurals.

- Write a list with plurals and possessive apostrophes mixed

Curriculum objectives

- To learn the possessive apostrophe (singular).
- To learn how to use both familiar and new punctuation correctly, including apostrophes for contracted forms and the possessive (singular).

Success criteria

- I understand that an apostrophe + 's' can show that something belongs to someone.
- I can use an apostrophe + 's' to show that something belongs to someone.

Apostrophes to show belonging

Learn

How else are apostrophes used?

An apostrophe can also be used to show that something belongs to someone.

We use an apostrophe + s to show that something belongs to someone.

Ellie's book

↑

apostrophe + s

the book belongs to Ellie

the dog's ball

↑

apostrophe + s

the ball belongs to the dog

Nouns ending in s are just the same!

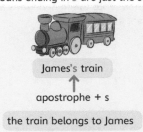

James's train

↑

apostrophe + s

the train belongs to James

the class's award

↑

apostrophe + s

the award belongs to the class

Plurals do **not** need an apostrophe.

We ate a lot of chocolates.

✓ Tip

If it belongs to something or someone, it needs an **apostrophe + s**!

up for the children to sort. Can they make up a rule to help them distinguish which is which?

• Dictate simple sentences using plurals and possessive apostrophes to check if the children have understood the concept.

• Use the activity 'Pirate Black's map' on page 97 of the *Year 2 Practice Book* to assess the children's understanding of apostrophes for possession and contraction.

• Use starter activity 9 in *100 English Lessons Year 2* (page 13) 'This belongs to…' to reinforce the concept.

• *The Year 2 Practice Book* explains how to use the possessive apostrophe and includes activities for practise.

Activities

1. **Copy each sentence. Add the missing apostrophe in the correct place.**

   a. We were woken up by the babys crying.

   b. I enjoyed playing with Mayas game.

   c. The footballers goal was very exciting.

   d. They were reading their favourite authors latest novel.

2. **Which sentences use apostrophes correctly? Write the correct sentence for each.**

   a. The cat's ate lots of food.   or   The cat's food had been eaten.
   b. The cake's were all sold.   or   The cake's filling was delicious.

3. **Who does it belong to? Work it out and then write the sentence.**

   a. Jamie's book
      the ____ belongs to ____

   b. the house's roof
      the ____ belongs to ____

   c. the giraffe's neck
      the ____ belongs to ____

   d. Miss Woodworth's pen
      the ____ belongs to ____

4. a. Choose a person in the picture. Choose an object for that person. Write who the object belongs to.

      For example: Gran's spade

   b. Write a sentence using one of the phrases you made in 4a.

Remember to use an **apostrophe + s.**

Punctuation **27**

Suffixes

Prior learning

- Terminology: adverb, noun, adjective, verb.
- Can spell root words mainly correctly.
- Can add suffixes to root words where no change is needed.

Learn

- Ensure children are familiar with the terms 'verb', 'adverb', 'noun' and 'adjective'.
- Explain that a suffix is a set of letters put at the end of a word to change its meaning. This word is often called a root word.

- Change adjectives to adverbs by adding 'ly'. Challenge the children to use these words. Draw their attention to how root words change (or not) when the suffix 'ly' is added. Show the children how they modify verbs.
- Create a list of nouns with the class. Add the suffixes 'ful' and 'less' to create adjectives. Use them to create expanded noun phrases describing a character's feelings or appearance.

- Create nouns using the suffixes 'ment' and 'ness'. Explain what happens to words ending in 'y' when the suffix 'ment' is added. There is additional support for this spelling rule in *Year 2 Practice Book* (page 39) 'It all adds up'.
- Encourage the children to find examples of words with these suffixes in texts.

Curriculum objectives

- To add suffixes to spell longer words, including 'ment', 'ness', 'ful', 'less', 'ly'.
- To form nouns using suffixes such as 'ness', 'er' and by compounding. (Grammar appendix)
- To form adjectives using suffixes such as 'ful', 'less'. (Grammar appendix)

Success criteria

- I understand that adding a suffix changes the meaning of the root word.
- I can form nouns by adding the suffixes 'ness' and 'ment'.
- I can form an adverb by adding the suffix 'ly' to an adjective.
- I can form adjectives by adding the suffixes 'ful' and 'less'.
- I can swap the 'y' for an 'i' when adding suffixes to words ending in 'y'.

Suffixes

Learn

What is a suffix?

A suffix is a set of letters you can put at the end of a word to change its meaning.

Here are some suffixes: ness   less   ment   fully

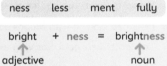

bright + ness = brightness
↑   ↑
adjective   noun

taste + less = tasteless
↑   ↑
noun   adjective

enjoy + ment = enjoyment
↑   ↑
verb   noun

care + ful = careful
↑   ↑
noun   adjective

To add a suffix to a word ending in y, change y to i.

plenty + ful = plentiful
↑   ↑
noun   adjective

Key words

suffix

✓ **Tip**

Adding a suffix changes the type of word.

You can add more than one suffix: care + ful + ly = carefully

- The textbook shows how root words change their class when the suffixes 'ment', 'ness', 'ful', 'less' and 'ly' are added. Children identify suffixes and practise adding them to words.

- **Note** the textbook introduces the swap the 'y' for 'i' rule for adding certain suffixes. This will need further practice with the *Year 2 Practice Book* and regular spelling activities.

- Give less confident learners extra practice by playing the interactive activity on the *100 English Lessons Year 2* CD-ROM 'Which suffix?'.

- There are numerous photocopiable sheets on the *100 English Lessons Year 2* CD-ROM that support children with adding suffixes and choosing appropriate suffixes.

- The *Year 2 Practice Book* activities explore how these suffixes change the word class and meaning of the root word.

Activities

1. Copy the words and then underline the suffix in each.

   amazement   handful   penniless   fondness

2. Choose a suffix for each word and write a new word.

ness	less	ment	ful

   move   tear   hope   sad

3. Add a different suffix to each word.

ment	ness	less	ful

   happy   merry   penny   beauty

4. Write sentences using the new words you made in question 3.

5. Change each adjective to an adverb by adding 'ly'.

   strong   soft   quick   safe

6. Change each adjective to an adverb by adding 'ly'.

   angry   busy   hungry   easy

You may need to change a letter.

Remember to change y to i before adding ly!

7. Choose two of your new adverbs and use them in a sentence.

8. Copy each verb and then write an adverb to describe each verb.
   For example: run quickly

verb	adverb
climb	
read	
swim	

9. Which suffix did you add to make your adverbs?

Suffixes: 'er' and 'est' and Suffixes: 'ed' and 'ing'

Prior learning

- Terminology: noun, adjective, verb.
- Can spell root words mainly correctly.
- Can add suffixes to root words where no change is needed.

Learn

- Ensure children are familiar with the terms 'verb', 'noun' and 'adjective'.
- Explain that a suffix is a set of letters put at the end of a word to change its meaning. This word is often called a root word.
- Explain how adding a suffix can change the word's class, and 'er' and 'est' are used to create adjectives. Show how the words change meaning incrementally with these suffixes: 'fast', 'faster', 'fastest'. Some words do not follow this sequence: 'good', 'better', 'best'. Orally rehearse sentences that use comparisons.
- Show how the ending of the root word can change when adding these suffixes: words end in 'y' (swap the 'y' for 'i'); words with a short vowel sound, then a single consonant (double the final letter); words ending in 'e' (drop the 'e'). Practise them all so that children can apply the correct rule confidently.

Curriculum objectives

- To use the suffixes 'er', 'est' in adjectives and 'ly' in Standard English to turn adjectives into adverbs. (Grammar appendix)
- To add 'ed', 'ing', 'er' and 'est' to a root word ending in 'y' with a consonant before it. (Spelling appendix)
- To add 'ing', 'ed', 'er', 'est' and 'y' to words ending in 'e' with a consonant before it. (Spelling appendix)
- To add 'ing', 'ed', 'er', 'est' and 'y' to words of one syllable ending in a single consonant after a single vowel. (Spelling appendix)

Success criteria

- I understand that adding a suffix changes the meaning of the root word.
- I can form adjectives by adding the suffixes 'er' and 'est'.
- I can form nouns by adding the suffix 'er'.
- I can 'swap double or drop' the final letter of the root word when adding a suffix.

Suffixes: 'er' and 'est'

Learn

How do we use the suffixes **er** and **est**?

er and **est** are suffixes. We use these suffixes to compare things.

For words with a long vowel sound in the middle we just add **er** or **est**:

tall   taller   tallest

For words ending in **e**, we lose the last **e** and then add **er** or **est**:

nice   nicer   nicest

For words ending in **y**, we change the **y** to **i** and then add **er** or **est**.

happy   happier   happiest

For words with a short vowel sound in the middle, we double the last letter:

sad   sadder   saddest

We can also add **er** to verbs to change them to nouns.

keep → keeper   teach → teacher
(verb) (noun)   (verb)   (noun)

✓ Tip

To compare **two** things, add **er**.

I am bigger than my brother.

To compare **three or more things**, add **est**.

My brother is the biggest boy in his class.

Activities

1. **Add 'er' and 'est' to each word to make two new words.**
   high   hot   heavy   wide

2. **Add a suffix to each verb to change it into a noun.**
   clean   build   bake

- The suffixes 'ing' and 'ed' are commonly used in the past and present verb tenses. Challenge children to find words with these endings and work out if the 'swap, double or drop' rule has been used, or if the root word has not been changed.

Activities

- The textbook activities show how to make comparative adjectives by adding 'er' and 'est' and how the suffix 'er' creates nouns such as 'teacher'. The suffixes 'ed' and 'ing' create verbs. Children identify suffixes and practise adding them to words.

- **Note** the textbook introduces rules for changing the end of the root word, which will need further practice. Use the *Year 2 Practice Book* and regular spelling activities.

- Less confident learners can practise with the photocopiable sheets on the *100 English Lessons Year 2* CD-ROM 'Practising suffixes' and 'Adding suffixes'.

- Support children by playing starter activity 10 'Add a suffix' from *100 English Lessons Year 2*. Begin with words that do not change when a suffix is added and slowly progress through the 'swap, double and drop' rules.

Suffixes: 'ed' and 'ing'

Learn

When do we use the suffixes **ed** and **ing**?

We use the suffixes ed and ing at the end of verbs.
Just add ed or ing:
cook + ed = cooked   cook + ing = cooking
The main word is not changed.

For verbs ending in e, just lose the end e and add ed or ing:
hike + ed = hiked   hike + ing = hiking

Only one **e**!

For verbs with a short vowel sound in the middle, you often double the last letter and then add ed or ing:
drop + ed = dropped   drop + ing = dropping

For verbs ending in y, change the y to i and add ed:
carry + ed = carried
BUT carry + ing = carrying
(Do not change the main word and + ing.)

Activities

1. Copy the verbs below and add 'ed' and 'ing' to each one. An example has been done for you.

	+ed	+ing
like	liked	liking
nod		
jump		
study		
joke		
cry		

100 English Lessons Year 2 links:

- Starter activity 10 (page 13): Add a suffix
- Spring 2, Week 5 (page 127): Lesson 1, What's it like
- Summer 1, Week 2 (page 151): Lesson 2, Revisiting suffixes

Year 2 Practice Book links:

- (page 19): Lose the 'e'
- (page 20): Root words
- (page 21): Drop the 'y' and add the 'i' (2)
- (page 22): What are they doing?
- (page 23): Doubling up
- (page 24): Double trouble
- (page 59): Add a suffix

Words ending with 'tion'

Prior learning

- Can read longer words with /shun/ endings.
- Can spell root words with confidence.
- Understand that a root word may change when an ending is added.

Learn

- The sound /shun/ can be written in a variety of ways ('cian', 'sion', 'ssion') but 'tion' is the most common.
- Some children will need support reading these longer words. Explain that the /shun/ sound is made up of the 'ti' which makes the /sh/ sound and 'o–n', which can be sounded out.
- Collect different words ending in 'tion' and talk about what they mean. Many words, such as 'question', 'exclamation', 'information' and 'instruction', will be familiar to the children. Ensure that they understand the meaning of new words by giving them examples in context.

- Ask children to explore which word classes 'tion' words belong to. (Words ending in 'tion' can be verbs and nouns.)
- Challenge children to use some of these words in their speech and writing.
- Show how the root word changes when 'tion' is added to it. (Drop the final letter in words ending in 't' or 'e').

Activities

- The textbook activities explain how to use the 'tion' spelling at the end of words. Children are encouraged to apply a simple 'drop the ending' rule for words ending in 't' and 'e' before adding 'tion'. These activities help them contextualise the new words in sentences.
- The *Year 2 Practice Book* has further activities to reinforce these spellings.

Curriculum objectives

- To spell words ending in 'tion'. (Spelling appendix)

Success criteria

- I can spell words ending with 'tion'.
- I know when to drop the final letter of the root word when adding 'tion'.

Year 2 Practice Book links:

- (page 46): Potion and lotion
- (page 47): Write and draw

Words ending with 'tion'

Learn

There are different ways to make words ending with a /shun/ sound. The most common way is with the letters tion.

These words all end with tion:

fiction   nation   position

Some words can have the suffix tion added:
  prevent + tion = prevention
  invent + tion = invention
lose the end t before adding tion

educate + tion = education
lose the end e before adding tion

Activities

1. a. Add 'tion' to these beginnings to make a word.

    ques___   ac___   addi___

  b. Write a sentence for each of your new words.

2. Copy these sentences and fill in the missing 'tion' words.

competition	subtraction	station	motion

  a. I caught a train from the ____.

  b. We entered the ____ and won a day at the theme park.

  c. The class are learning ____ of pairs of two–digit numbers.

  d. The car's ____ made him feel ill.

3. Choose a book. How many words can you find which end with 'tion'? Make a list. Can you use each word in a sentence?

Long vowel sounds

Prior learning

- Can read the alternate spelling of the long vowel sounds.
- Can spell the most common graphemes for long vowel sounds.

Learn

- Review the different ways that the long vowel sounds /ai/, /ee/, /igh/ and /oo/ can be spelled.
- Challenge the children to find examples of words spelled with each of the different graphemes.

- Use rhyming poetry to help children see how words can rhyme but not have the same spelling.

Activities

- The textbook activities can be easily expanded to include further graphemes that represent the long vowel sounds.
- *100 English Lessons Year 2* uses rhyming poetry as a context for exploring the different spellings of the long vowel sounds. Ask children to look out for further examples in poems they read.
- The *Year 2 Practice Book* provides further support for the spelling of common homophones and uses sentences and labelling activities to help children contextualise these words.

Curriculum objectives

- To learn new ways of spelling phonemes for which one or more spellings are already known, and to learn some words with each spelling, including homophones.

Success criteria

- I can choose which spelling to use when writing words with long vowel sounds.
- I can choose the correct homophone to use in a sentence.

100 English Lessons Year 2 links:

- Autumn 2, Week 6 (pages 66–68): the long vowel sound spelled differently
- Summer 2, Week 3 (pages 185–187): the long vowel sound spelled differently, including a few common homophones

Year 2 Practice Book links:

- (page 15): The dry spy
- (page 29): Barney's honey
- (page 48): Snap!
- (page 49): Sounds like…
- (page 50): Pick the word
- (page 51): In the garden

Long vowel sounds

Learn

What is a long vowel sound?

Vowels are the letters **a**, **e**, **i**, **o** and **u**.

A long vowel sound is a sound which sounds like the letter's name.

There are many ways to make one sound.

Long /a/ sound	Long /e/ sound	Long /i/ sound	Long /o/ sound	Long /u/ sound
make	these	five	home	tube
day	feet	night	road	new
rain	field	pie	bowl	
	read			

✓ Tip

Try to learn spellings in groups like these.

night	field	road	brain
fight	chief	toad	paid
sight	grief	coach	afraid
delight	thief	goal	wait

Activities

1. **Copy the sentences. Then underline all the long /e/ sounds.**

   a. We went to the beach to see the sand.

   b. The chief raised the green flag completely.

2. **Choose and copy the correct spelling for each word.**

   a. frite   friet   fright

   b. cube   cewb   cueb

   c. sheeld   shield   sheald

   Key words
   vowels
   long vowel sound

Spelling **33**

Tricky vowel sounds: /or/ and /air/

Prior learning

- Can read words with the different /or/ and /air/ graphemes.

Learn

- There is more than one way to write the sounds /or/ and /air/. Ask the children to think of words with the /or/ or /air/ sound and make a list of them on the board. Ensure all the spellings are included, and underline each different one. These include /or/:

Curriculum objectives

- To learn new ways of spelling phonemes for which one or more spellings are already known, and to learn some words with each spelling, including a few common homophones.

Success criteria

- I can choose which spelling of the /or/ and /air/ sound to use.
- I can recognise an /or/ or an /air/ word that is spelled incorrectly.

100 English Lessons Year 2 links:

- Autumn 2, Week 6 (pages 66–68): explore the spellings of /or/ words that rhyme
- Summer 2, Week 3 (pages 185–187): understand that rhyming words may have different spellings

Year 2 Practice Book links:

- (page 25): Colour the ball
- (page 26): /or/ word search
- (page 33): The warthog's wardrobe

'or', 'oor', 'au', 'ore', 'aw', 'a', 'ar' and /air/: 'air', 'are', 'ear', 'ere'.

- Draw attention to words that are homophones such as 'paw' and 'poor', 'fare' and 'fair', 'stare' and 'stair', 'wear' and 'where'.
- Create lists of rhyming words with the /or/ and /air/ sounds and explore how the spelling of these sounds is not always the same. Does the position of the /air/ or /or/ sound impact the rhyme or how the sound is spelled?

Activities

- The textbook activity explores some spellings of the sounds /or/ and /air/.
- Children choose the correct spelling of a word to complete a sentence.
- Children choose from two homophones to complete a sentence. Challenge children to write their own versions of this activity.

Tricky vowel sounds: /or/ and /air/

Learn

What is tricky about the vowel sounds /or/ and /air/?

The vowel sounds /or/ and /air/ can be tricky because they can be spelled in lots of different ways.

or	au	ore	aw	oor
for	caught	more	saw	door
short	author	score	jaw	poor
born	August	before	yawn	floor

air	ere
fair	there
stair	where
chair	nowhere

are	ear
bare	bear
fare	wear
scared	pear

Some of these words sound the same, but have a different spelling.

fair   **fare**

Different spelling = different meaning

✓ Tip

Be careful! The letters ear can make a different sound, as in wear and fear.

Activities

1. **Write each sentence. Choose the bold word that is spelled correctly.**

   a. My teacher **tort / taught / tawt** me about Florence Nightingale.

   b. **Dinosores / Dinosaws / Dinosaurs** lived millions of years ago.

   c. My little sister has begun to **crorl / craul / crawl**.

   d. I cuddle my teddy **bear / bare** in bed.

   e. We picked **pairs / pears** off the tree.

The /o/ sound after 'w' and 'qu'

Prior learning

- Can read words with the /o/ sound spelled 'a' after 'w' and 'qu'.

Learn

- Many people (even adults) find spelling these words hard because the grapheme 'a' is pronounced (in some words) as /o/ after a 'w' or a 'qu.' The 'qu' words originate in Greek and Latin.

- Create lists of words that have the 'wa' and 'qua' spelling patterns and see if they all follow the 'a' says /o/ rule. (There are a few exceptions, such as 'wag', 'wax' and 'quack'.)

- Use the 'say it silly' strategy to say the word as it is spelled, so that children can write these words accurately.

- Children often misspell the common exception words 'what', 'want' and 'watch'. They use these words a lot so it is harder for the correct spelling to gain traction. Help them break this habit by placing these words on 'high alert': write them in a 'high alert' box and point out the correct spelling. Use chants and 'say it silly' to implant the correct spelling then practise these words until the correct spelling becomes second nature. Then assign a few new words to the 'high alert' list.

Activities

- The textbook activities explain why the grapheme 'a' makes the /o/ sound after the letters 'w' and 'qu'. It helps children understand the meaning of the words as well as how to spell them.

- *The Year 2 Practice Book* activities can be used to reinforce these spelling patterns.

The /o/ sound after 'w' and 'qu'

Learn

How is the /o/ sound after **w** or **qu** made?

Words with **w** or **qu** often have an /o/ sound (as in **hot**) in the middle.

The /o/ sound is made with an a.

was	squad
what	quantity

If you see a word with a **w** or **qu** in it, you know the middle a sounds like /o/!

Activities

1. Draw each picture and write the correct word for it underneath.

2. Copy each sentence and write the correct 'w' or 'qu' word in each space.

wash	squad	watch	want	squash

   a. I ____ a drink, please.

   b. Go and ____ your hands and face.

   c. Ali was in the football ____ for this season's games.

   d. You will need to ____ the boxes before putting them in the bin.

   e. My ____ says it is ten o'clock.

3. Write each definition with the correct word next to it.

quantity	squat	quarrel	quality

   a. a crouching position
   b. something of value
   c. argument
   d. a number of things

Curriculum objectives

- To spell the /o/ sound spelled 'a' after 'w' and 'qu'. (Spelling appendix)

Success criteria

- I can spell words with the /o/ sound spelled 'a' after 'w' and 'qu'.

100 English Lessons Year 2 links:

- Starter activity (page 14): Spelling bingo

Year 2 Practice Book links:

- (page 30): Squish squash
- (page 31): Find the path

Tricky endings: 'le' or 'el', 'al' or 'il'?

Prior learning

- Terminology: vowel, consonant.
- Can hear the sounds in words.

Learn

- The /l/ sound is very tricky as there is little to distinguish the spelling of the sound at the end of a word. However, there are some generalisations that can help children to spell this sound accurately.

- Start by investigating the different spellings of the /l/ sound at the end of words. Make a list /l/ words using the spellings 'le', 'il', 'al' and 'el' on an A4 sheet of paper. Make copies and ask the children to cut them out and order them (in any way they see fit). Discuss their findings. Ask them to sort the words looking at the /l/ spelling. Can they see any patterns that would help them predict which ending to use in a word?

- The most common spelling of the /l/ sound is 'le'. Challenge children to make a collection of words with this spelling. Ask them to note any other spelling pattern that they notice within these words. (Words with a short vowel sound followed by a consonant double the consonant before adding the 'le', such as 'apple', 'middle', 'little').

Curriculum objectives

- To spell the /l/ or /ul/ sound spelled 'le', 'el' and 'al' at the end of words. (Spelling appendix)
- To spell words ending 'il'. (Spelling appendix)

Success criteria

- I can choose the correct spelling of the /l/ sound at the end of words.

Tricky endings: 'le' or 'el', 'al' or 'il'?

Learn

What is tricky about these endings?

The endings le, el, al and il all sound the same, so it can be tricky to know which one to use.

More common ending		Less common ending
le	or	el
apple table little		tunnel parcel travel
more common ending		used after m, n, r, s, v, w and often after s or c
al	or	il
pedal metal animal		pencil fossil nostril

✓ Tip

Say each word and exaggerate the end sound to help you learn the spelling.
tab-le   tunn-el   met-al   penc-il
Remember: **le** and **al** are the most common endings.

Activities

1. **Write the correct spelling for each word.**
   a. squirral   sqirrel   squirrle   squirrel
   b. camle   camel   camal   camil
   c. capital   capitil   capetal   capitel

2. **Use each word in a sentence.**

- The letters 'm', 'n', 'r', 'v', 'w' (and often 's' or 'c') come before the ending 'el'. This is a less common spelling than 'le'. Challenge children to find out if this rule always works (it won't always work for 's').

- Words ending in 'al' are less common than both of the preceding spellings of /l/. 'al' can be used as a suffix to make adjectives, such as 'tidal' and 'comical'. Most of the root words in the activities are nouns.

- Challenge the children to find more words ending in 'al' and sort them into adjectives or nouns.

- The least common spelling of /l/ is 'il'. Children won't need to spell many of these words except for 'pencil' and 'fossil'. Words ending 'il' often come from French or Latin. Some children may enjoy finding more 'il' words and discovering their meaning and origins.

Activities

- The textbook clearly outlines information about the four spellings of the /l/ sound, and identifies which is the most common spelling. Children learn to recognise the correct spelling of /l/ words and use them in context.

- There are several activities in the *Year 2 Practice Book* to help children learn the four /l/ spellings. Repeated practice of reading and writing these tricky endings will help cement the spelling patterns in children's minds.

- Some children will need extra practice. Get them to write /l/ words using a different colour for each ending.

Write

- Use the information from the activities above to make a class poster that helps children decide which spelling of /l/ to use. Children can organise their poster in various ways, such as a decision tree, a series of questions or information with examples.

3. **Write each sentence. Choose the correct word for each space.**

> tunnel   fossil   pedal   bottle

a. The baby's _____ was full of milk.

b. The train went through the dark _____.

c. They collected a very old _____ from the seashore.

d. We had to _____ hard to get our bikes up the hill.

4. **Copy the table below.**

a. Write each word into the correct box.

> apple   tunnel   pencil   camel
> travel   nostril   hospital   middle   towel
> fossil   tinsel   animal   table

al	el	il	le

b. Find more words to add to these groups.

Learn the words in these groups.

5. **Search through fiction and non-fiction books to find your own words with 'al', 'el', 'il' or 'le' endings. List them in each group to help you learn them.**

Spelling   37

100 English Lessons Year 2 links:

- Starter activity 14 (page 14): 'le' or 'el'

Year 2 Practice Book links:

- (page 11): Puddle muddle
- (page 12): Table labels
- (page 13): Camels and squirrels
- (page 14): What's the ending?

Tricky endings: 'dge' or 'ge'?

Prior learning

- Terminology: vowel, consonant.
- Can identify short and long vowel sounds in words.

Learn

- The graphemes 'dge' and 'ge' make the /dj/ sound. Explain that 'dge' appears in words with a short vowel sound. Say that 'dge' protects the short vowel sound in these words.
- The grapheme 'ge' appears when there is a long vowel sound ('huge') or where the short vowel sound is already protected by a consonant ('change').

Curriculum objectives

- To spell the /dj/ sound spelled as 'ge' and 'dge' at the end of words, and sometimes spelled as 'g' elsewhere in words before 'e', 'i' and 'y'. (Spelling appendix)

Success criteria

- I know when to use 'dge' or 'ge' at the end of a word.
- I can spell words using 'g' to spell the /dj/ sound.

100 English Lessons Year 2 links:

- Spring 1, Week 2 (page 87): Lesson 3, Follow the rules
- Summer 1, Week 6 (page 163): Lesson 2, Just like a /j/

Year 2 Practice Book links:

- (page 6): Sort the /j/ sound
- (page 7): Write and draw

Collect and sort 'dge' and 'ge' words. Can children identify the long and short vowels? Do all the words follow the rule?

- Challenge children to find words containing the grapheme 'g' and investigate what sound it makes. Can they work out why the grapheme changes its sound? It makes a different sound when followed by 'i', 'e' and 'y' ('giant', 'gem' and 'gym').

Activities

- In the textbook, children sort words according to the spelling rule and choose the correct spelling.
- Use the photocopiable sheet in *100 English Lessons Year 2* (page 175) 'Just like a /j/' and the interactive activity on the CD-ROM 'Which /j/?' to support children.

Tricky endings: 'dge' or 'ge'?

Learn

What is tricky about these endings?

The endings dge and ge sound the same, so it can be tricky to know which one to use.

ledge   fudge   bridge

Use dge after a **short vowel sound**.

age   change   huge

Use ge after all other sounds.

short vowel sounds:
a as cat   e as in egg   i as in bin
o as in cot   u as in but

✓ **Tip**

Never use j at the end of a word.

Activities

1. Write these 'dge' and 'ge' words. Say them aloud and then tick the words which have short vowel sounds.

ledge   page   badge   charge   dodge

2. Write the word with the correct spelling in each pair.

a. stage / stadge   c. strange / strandge

b. lardge / large   d. juge / judge

Tricky letter pairs: 'kn', 'gn' and 'wr'

Prior learning

- Can read and identify the most common graphemes for the /n/ and /r/ sounds.

Learn

- Make cards of words with and without silent letters. Ask children to sort them. Can they identify the words that don't have silent letters?

- Support children to spell words with silent letters by teaching them to say the silent letter in the word before they spell it. By 'saying it silly', children can embed the spelling pattern. Make up silly sentences using silent letter words. Ask the children to repeat each sentence after you. Emphasise the silent letter as you read: 'I k-now you k-nead bread with your k-nuckles!'

- Some of these words are homophones. Make a list of them, for instance 'night' and 'knight', and help the children to think how they can distinguish them.

Activities

- The textbook lists some common silent letter words with the graphemes 'wr', 'gn' and 'kn'.
- Use the *Year 2 Practice Book* to consolidate children's knowledge.
- Support children by getting them to make posters for each silent letter. Help them create lists of words and then highlight the silent letter.

Tricky letter pairs: 'kn', 'gn' and 'wr'

Learn

What is tricky about kn, gn and wr?

These pairs of letters are tricky because one letter in each pair is a silent letter.

A silent letter is a letter you can't hear when you say the word.

kn	gn	wr
↑	↑	↑
silent k	silent g	silent w
know	gnome	wrist
knee	gnat	wrong
knot	gnash	wrap

✓ Tip

To help spell these words, sound-out the silent letter.

Key words

silent letter

Activities

1. **Write out these words and colour the silent letter in each.**

   write   knob   gnaw   knife

2. **Copy each clue and write the answer next to it. Spell each word correctly.**

Clue	Word
To use needles and wool to make clothes	
A ship at the bottom of the sea	
To chew	

Curriculum objectives

- To spell the /n/ sound spelled 'kn' and (less often) 'gn' at the beginning of words. (Spelling appendix)
- To spell the /r/ sound spelled 'wr' at the beginning of words. (Spelling appendix)

Success criteria

- I can spell words with silent letters for the /n/ sound 'kn' and 'gn'.
- I can spell words with silent letters for the /r/ sound 'wr'.

100 English Lessons Year 2 links:

- Starter activity (page 14): 'wr' quiz
- Spring 2, Week 3 (page 122): Lesson 2, Knees and knuckles

Year 2 Practice Book links:

- (page 9): Do you know the word?
- (page 10): Shipwreck

The soft 'c' sound

Prior learning

- Can read words with alternate graphemes for the /s/ sound.

Learn

- When the grapheme 'c' makes the sound /s/, it is known as the soft 'c' sound. This happens when 'e' or 'i' follow the letter 'c'.
- Write lists of words that include the letter 'c'. Ask the children to read them and sort them according to how the 'c' is pronounced. Challenge the children to work out why the 'c' in some words makes the /s/ sound. Explain the soft 'c' rule and ask the children to see if they can find more words that follow the rule.
- Challenge children to find the soft 'c' in multi-syllabic words such as 'acceptance'. Does the soft 'c' rule still apply?

Activities

- The textbook outlines the soft 'c' rule and gives children example words to read and sort.
- The activity in the *Year 2 Practice Book* extends the rule to include words where 'c' is followed by 'y'. Ask children to find other examples of words that follow this pattern to extend the activity.

Curriculum objectives

- To spell the /s/ sound spelled 'c' before 'e', 'i' and 'y'. (Spelling appendix)

Success criteria

- I can spell words where the /s/ sound is spelled 'c'.

100 English Lessons Year 2 links:

- Starter activity 12 (page 14): 's' or 'c'?

Year 2 Practice Book links:

- (page 8): Ice race

The soft 'c' sound

What is the soft **c** sound?

Learn

A **soft c** sounds like an **/s/** as in **sun**.

race   ice   cell   city

These all sound like **/s/** (as in **sun**). They usually have **i** or **e** after them.

> There are other words with ace or ice hiding in them:
> face and space or mice and price.
> Can you think of others?

Activities

1. Copy the table. Sort the words into the two groups.

spicy	camel	cinema	picture
camera	camping	pencil	

Soft c	Not soft c

In adjectives soft **c** is often followed by **y**. For example, fancy.

2. Copy each sentence. Finish the missing words.
   a. The curry was very sp___.
   b. My pe___ needs sharpening.
   c. She will need to take a spoon of medi___ three times daily.
   d. Every sent___ starts with a capital letter.

40   Spelling

Tricky 's' endings

Prior learning

- Can read words ending in 'sure' and 'sion'.

Learn

- The 's' in the endings 'sure' and 'sion' makes a /zh/ sound.
- Many of these words are multi-syllabic. Ensure the children can read them confidently before learning to spell them.
- Tell the children they are going to be sound detectives, looking for the /zh/ sound. Write /zh/ spelled 's' words on the board. Ask the children to read them (the words will end in 'sure' or 'sion'). Break the words into syllables and ask the children to identify which letter(s) make the /zh/ sound. Circle the 's' in each word.
- Ask the children to help you collect more 'sion' and 'sure' words.
- Draw attention to how these words are spelled when you use them during modelled writing.

Activities

- Use the textbook to introduce the /zh/ sound spelled 's' in words. Extend the activity by adding to the list of word beginnings for children to add the endings 'sion' or 'sure' to.
- Use the *Year 2 Practice Book* activities to help children identify words with the /zh/ sound.
- Support children reading these words by teaching them how to read the endings 'sion' and 'sure' before they try to read and spell them independently.

Tricky 's' endings

Learn

What **s** endings are tricky?

Some s endings are tricky because the **s** doesn't sound like /s/ as in **sun**.

television   treasure   usual

Say these words. The s in each word sounds the same. There are lots of words with this sound.

Look for words ending with sion or sure. They will have this sound. The s may be followed by u as in usual.

Activities

1. **Write two more words with the same ending as each word below.**

   television   treasure

2. **Choose the correct ending for each beginning to make a word. Write the words you make.**

Beginning	+ 'sion' or 'sure'?
confu	
plea	
divi	
mea	
in	
explo	
un	
deci	

Curriculum objectives

- To spell the /zh/ sound spelled 's'. (Spelling appendix)

Success criteria

- I can spell words that end with 'sure' and 'sion'.

Year 2 Practice Book links:

- (page 34): Treasure words
- (page 35): Alien landing!

Making a long /i/ sound at the end of a word

Prior learning

- Can read alternate spellings of /igh/.
- Can read words that end in /igh/ spelled 'y'.

Learn

- The spelling 'y' is often used when the /igh/ sound is at the end of a word.
- The spelling 'ie' making the /igh/ sound at the end of a word is less common.
- The spelling 'igh' can be used to make the /igh/ sound in the middle and at the end of words.
- Challenge the class to think of as many words ending in /igh/ as they can. Write a list and sort according to the spelling 'igh', 'y' and 'ie'. Which list is the longest?
- Children will find it easy to think of single syllable words ending in 'y'. Challenge them to think of longer words, such as 'July' and 'reply'.
- Extend children to add suffixes to words ending in the /igh/ sound. Do they need to swap, double or drop?

Curriculum objectives

- To spell the /igh/ sound spelled 'y' at the end of words. (Spelling appendix)

Success criteria

- I can spell words with the /igh/ sound spelled 'y' at the end of words.

Year 2 Practice Book links:

- (page 15): The dry spy

Activities

- Extend the textbook activity by asking children to use the long /i/ words there to write silly sentences.
- Extend the children's understanding of the sounds the letter 'y' can make by giving them words ending in 'y' that have the sounds /igh/ or /ee/ to sort.

Write

- Collect words that have the /igh/ sound at the end of the word. See how many different spellings there are. Write silly tongue twisters as a class. Challenge children to think of words that end in /igh/ and start with the same sound, such as 'fry' and 'fly' and use these to make your tongue twister even more twisted!

Making a long /i/ sound at the end of a word

Learn

How do you make a long /i/ sound at the end of a word?

One way to make a long /i/ sound (as in **high**) at the end of a word is to use y.

All these words have a long /i/ sound at the end:

cry   shy   reply   deny

Often the words have one syllable or part.

Sometimes the long /i/ sound at the end of a word is made using **ie**.

pie   tie

Activities

1. **Read the text below. Then list all the words which use 'y' to make a long /i/ sound.**

   The kitten began to cry loudly. It was very shy and tried to hide away. I started to try to pick her up but she was too sly.

2. **Make new words that end with the long /i/ sound. Write them down. For example:** pie

   There are only a few words which use **ie** at the end to make a long /i/ sound. Most words use **y**!

   sp___   t___
   fl___   l___
   Jul___   d___
   sk___   multipl___

Using 'ey' to make an /ee/ sound

Prior learning

- Can read words with alternate spellings of the /ee/ sound.

Learn

- The most common spelling of /ee/ at the end of a word is 'y'. Less commonly, the sound /ee/ at the end of words is sometimes spelled 'ey'.

- Challenge the class to think of as many words ending in /ee/ as they can. Write a list and sort according to the spelling 'ee', 'y', 'ey' and 'ea'. Which list is the longest?
- Draw attention to the words ending in 'ey'. These words are often nouns and have two syllables.

Activities

- The textbook activities explore two different spellings of the /ee/ sound, 'ey' and 'y', at the end of words. Children unjumble 'ey' words and use some 'ey' words in context.
- As there are a limited number of words that end in 'ey' making the sound /ee/, it is worth helping children learn a list of them, rather than trying to find a rule to follow.

Write

- Using a list of /ee/ words sorted into their different spellings, make up silly sentences using as many of these words as possible.

Using 'ey' to make an /ee/ sound

Learn

When do we use **ey** to make an /**ee**/ sound?

Most words just use y to make an /**ee**/ sound at the end of a word.

happy   funny   Mummy   Daddy   Gregory

The /**ee**/ sound at the end of someone's name is often made with y or ie.

Some words make the /**ee**/ sound with ey at the end. You need to learn these.

donkey   money   valley

Remember to end each word with **ey**.

Activities

1. **Use the clues to help you unjumble these words. Copy each clue and write down each unjumbled word.**

Clue	Word	Clue	Word
A herb	aprsely	It's often eaten at Christmas	krutey
A trip	ojureny	It is used to put shopping in	yolltre
An organ in the body	dikyne	Land between hills	lavely
Bees make it	yenoh		

2. **Copy the sentences and fill in the missing words.**

jockey   money   chimney   Monkeys

a. I have been saving ____ to buy a new game.
b. ____ live in hot countries and can be very naughty.
c. The ____ rode the horse fast over the jumps.
d. There was smoke coming out of the ____.

Spelling **43**

Curriculum objectives

- To spell the /ee/ sound spelled 'ey'. (Spelling appendix)

Success criteria

- I can spell words with the /ee/ sound spelled 'ey'.

100 English Lessons Year 2 links:

- Starter activity 15 (page 14): Spelling bingo

Year 2 Practice Book links:

- (page 29): Barney's honey

The /or/ sound before 'l' and 'll'

Prior learning

- Can read words with the /or/ sound spelled 'a' before 'l' and 'll'.
- Can identify the /or/ sound in words.

Learn

Learn

- The sound /or/ is usually spelled 'a' before the letters 'l' and 'll'. Common examples are 'ball', 'call', 'always', 'walk' and 'talk'.
- Help children identify this sound in the words as they read them. Ask them to tell you what sound the 'a' is making in the words.

- Collect words with 'a' before 'l' from texts, such as 'halt', 'talk', 'stalk', 'chalk'. Explore which letters come after the 'l'.
- Some words do not follow the rule: remind children of words that end in 'al' such as 'petal'. The 'a' makes the /u/ sound here. Can the children think of other words that end with the spelling 'al'?

Activities

- Use the textbook to help children generate words that end in 'all'. Extend the activity by challenging them to generate multi-syllabic words or compound words using the 'all' words they have made.
- Use the *Year 2 Practice Book* activities for children who need to practise identifying the /or/ sound in words.

Curriculum objectives

- To spell the /or/ sound spelled 'a' before 'l' and 'll'. (Spelling appendix)

Success criteria

- I can spell words with the /or/ sound spelled 'a' before 'l' and 'll'.

Year 2 Practice Book links:

- (page 25): Colour the ball
- (page 26): /or/ word search

The /or/ sound before 'l' and 'll'

Learn

How do you make the /or/ sound before l and ll?

To make the /or/ sound (as in **for**) before l and ll, you just use a.

Before l		
walk	talk	always

Before ll			
all	fall	wall	stall

a + l or a + ll = /or/ sound (as in **for**)

✓ Tip

Watch out! Some words have a silent l.

Activities

1. a b c d e f g h i j k l m n o p q r s t u v w x y z

   Use the alphabet above to help you make words ending with 'all'. The first ones have been done for you.

   all, ball, ____

2. **Copy these sentences and fill in the missing 'al' or 'all' words.**

   | nightfall | small | walk | holdall | all |

   a. After a long ____ we needed to clean our muddy boots.

   b. Our dog has just had three ____ puppies.

   c. As the sun went down we waited for ____.

   d. The children put their swimming things into a large ____.

   e. We ____ read every evening after tea.

Using 'o' to make a short /u/ sound

Prior learning

- Can read examples of these words, many of which are common exception words.
- Can identify short vowel sounds in words.

Learn

- The letter 'o' often makes the short vowel sound /u/ when it is followed by 'n', 'v' and 'th'.
- Ensure the children can read the words, some of which are in the common exception words list for Year 1 in the Spelling appendix of the curriculum.
- Many of the words with this spelling pattern are common words. Ensure your children don't over-learn the incorrect spelling. Make lists of words with this spelling pattern for them to read and refer to when they are writing. Draw attention to these words when you are modelling writing; ask children to tell you how to spell these words, or use their whiteboards to spell them for you before you write. Use the 'say it silly' strategy to highlight the 'o' grapheme.

Activities

- Use the *Year 2 Practice Book* activities to help children identify words with the /u/ sound spelled 'o'.
- Extend the sorting activity in the textbook by using additional words that have the same spelling pattern.

Using 'o' to make a short /u/ sound

When do you use **o** to make a short /u/ sound?

Learn

Monday   brother   mother

o in these words = /u/ sound (as in **but**)

This short /u/ sound often comes before n, v or th.

✓ Tip

Remember, the short /u/ sound can be made with an o, as in mother.

Activities

1. **Read the text below. Then copy out all the words which use 'o' to make a short /u/ sound.**

   Every month, my brother loves to come and play with me. My mother covers the table with a cloth and we have a lovely meal. When we are done, we all have some tea to drink.

2. a. Copy the table and write each word into the correct box.

love	some	money	month	above
front	dozen	govern	cover	nothing
dove	monkey	another		

Short /u/ sound before 'n'	Short /u/ sound before 'v'	Short /u/ sound before 'th'

   b. Two words did not belong in the table above. What were they? Write two sentences, using each of these words.

Curriculum objectives

- To spell the /u/ sound spelled 'o'. (Spelling appendix)

Success criteria

- I can spell words with the /u/ sound spelled 'o'.

Year 2 Practice Book links:

- (page 27): Word trees
- (page 28): I love sandcastles!

Making an /or/ sound after 'w' and Making an /ur/ sound after 'w'

Prior learning

- Understand that sounds can be spelled with alternative graphemes.
- Can identify the sounds in words, especially the long vowel sounds.

Learn

- The letter 'w' in words often changes how the letters after it sound. This is sometimes called the 'w special' rule. When the letters 'or' come after 'w' they make the sound /ur/ ('worm'). When the letters 'ar' come after 'w' they make the sound /or/ ('warm').

- Start investigating this rule by making lists of words with 'war' or 'wor' in them. Ask children to read the words and sort them by the sounds that directly follow the letter 'w'. You could extend this activity to include other words that follow the 'w special' rule, for example, /wo/ spelled as 'wa'.
- Play games where children have to distinguish 'war' (/wor/) words from 'wa' (/wo/) words.

Curriculum objectives

- To spell the /ur/ sound spelled 'or' after 'w'. (Spelling appendix)
- To spell the /or/ sound spelled 'ar' after 'w'. (Spelling appendix)

Success criteria

- I can spell words with the /ur/ sound spelled 'or' after the letter 'w'.
- I can spell words with the /or/ sound spelled 'ar' after the letter 'w'.

Making an /or/ sound after 'w'

Learn

How do you make an /or/ sound after **w**?

To make an /or/ sound (as in **for**) after w, you can use ar.

war   ward

There are not many of these words, so it's best to just learn them.

Activities

1. **Add 'ar' to these letters to make words. Write each one down.**

   w___den   w___rmest

   w___ped   w___drobe

2. **Copy each sentence. Choose the best word to fill each space.**

warns	warmth	warships	warden

   a. Europe has sent some _____ to the Mediterranean Sea.

   b. The lighthouse _____ ships that they are near rocks.

   c. The _____ in the Nature Reserve showed us how to pond dip.

   d. We enjoyed the sun's _____ as we played on the beach.

3. **Write four sentences using the words below.**

warble	warped	warlike	ward

✓ Tip

If you can spell **war** you can spell all of these words and more!

- Write 'worry', 'worse', 'work' and 'sword' on the board. Can the children read the words and work out which have the /ur/ sound?

- Show the children that words with the split vowel digraph 'a–e' ('ware') do not make the /wor/ sound.

- Ensure children can read these words accurately and draw attention to the unusual spelling of words that follow the 'w special' rule when you find them in texts.

- Make a wanted poster of the most difficult common misspellings of these words. Words such as 'swap', 'worth' and 'wonder' even cause adults trouble!

Activities

- Use the textbook to explore why the graphemes 'ar' and 'or' make different sounds after the letter 'w'.

- Practise these spelling patterns further using the *Year 2 Practice Book* activities.

- Help children remember these unusual spelling patterns by making posters of the words, by encouraging them to say the words silly when they spell them ('w-ar') and by highlighting the graphemes that the 'w' changes.

Making an /ur/ sound after 'w'

How do you make an /ur/ sound after **w**?

Learn

To make an /ur/ sound (as in **fur**) after w, you can use or.

word   work

There are not many of these words, which makes it easier to learn them!

Activities

1. **Use the clues to help you unjumble these words. Copy each clue and write down each unjumbled word.**

Clue	Word
A male who does a job.	anwmkro
The Earth and everything on it.	rdlow
A piece of paper with tasks on it.	theesorwk
A long creature which lives in soil.	rowm
A group of letters with meaning.	drow

2. a. Choose 'or' or 'ar' to complete these words. Some of the words could take either spelling.

    w__rkers   w__ning   w__se   aw__ded

    w__med   w__ldly   w__ship   w__ked

    b. Choose two words from above and write a sentence for each one.

3. a. How many 'or' words can you find on the warship? List each word.

    b. Look at your list. Which word does not use 'or' to make an /ur/ sound?

WARLORD   WORKFORCE   WORD
WARDROBE   WARMEST   WORMED
WORSEN   WORN

Spelling **47**

100 English Lessons Year 2 links:

- Starter activity 15 (page 14): Spelling bingo

Year 2 Practice Book links:

- (page 32): A world of fish

- (page 33): The warthog's wardrobe

Tricky words

Prior learning

- Can read words in the Year 1 and Year 2 common exception words list.

Learn

- Common exception words for Year 2 children are listed in the Spelling appendix of the curriculum.
- Use strategies such as 'say it silly' to say words as they are spelled ('h-al-f', 'pr-e-tty').

Curriculum objectives

- To learn to spell common exception words.

Success criteria

- I can break up words and identify the unusual spelling patterns.

100 English Lessons Year 2 links:

- Autumn 2, Week 3 (pages 57–59): highlight common exception words
- Autumn 2, Week 6 (pages 66–68): spell homophones including some common exception words
- Summer 1, Week 4 (page 157): Lesson 2, Some tricky words
- Summer 2, Week 6 (page 194): Lesson 1, Confident writers
- Summer 2, Assess and review (page 197): Common exception words

Year 2 Practice Book links:

- (page 52–8): Look, cover, say, write!

- Help children find words they can already spell within the tricky word (w-ant, w-hat, man-y).
- Use mnemonics to learn some words. 'Would', 'could' and 'should' all have the same spelling pattern; O U Lucky Duck!
- Together, sort similar words and learn them ('move', 'improve' and 'prove'; 'grass', 'class' and 'pass'). Write the tricky bit in a different colour so it stands out.

Activities

- The textbook activity explores the strategy of breaking up the tricky word into syllables and identifying the unusual graphemes. Children can then think of a way to remember the tricky part of the word. Extend this strategy to help children spell other common exception words.
- Use the photocopiable sheet on the *100 English Lessons Year 2* CD-ROM 'Common exception words' to practise using these words in context.

Tricky words

What are tricky words?

Learn

Tricky words may be longer words or words with unusual spelling patterns.

> **✓ Tip**
>
> Split tricky words into parts. Is there a root word?
> Look for unusual spelling patterns. Can you think of other words with the same pattern?

Tricky words are easier to spell if we split them into parts.

children = child + ren ← Learn ild in child.

everybody = every + body ← There is very in every.

beautiful = beauty + ful ← Change end y to i. Add ful. Learn eau in beauty.

Activities

1. **Copy these words and split each one into parts.**
   a. friendly
   c. improve
   b. behind
   d. people

2. **Write any unusual spelling patterns that you find in the words above.**

3. **Use each of these words in a sentence.**
   a. others
   b. because
   c. clothes

48   Spelling

Compound words

Prior learning

- Terminology: adjective, noun, suffix, verb.

Learn

- Joining two words together, often two nouns, creates a new word called a compound word. Many common words have been made in this way. In general, the two words just join together without any fuss!

- Ask the children to help you write lists of nouns. How many of them can be combined to make new words?

- Some pronouns are compound words as well, such as 'yourself', 'myself', 'everybody'. Show children how these words are created and check they understand what they mean. (Note children do not need to know the term 'pronoun'.)

- New compound words are created all the time to name new things. Challenge the children to find new compound words. The worlds of science, technology and journalism are good areas to go looking!

Activities

- The textbook starts an exploration of compound words, which you can easily extend.

- Use the starter activities in *100 English Lessons Year 2* to consolidate grammar terminology and make compound words.

Compound words

Learn

What are compound words?

Compound words are made up of two or more other words.

Two or more words can be put together to make one new word.

motor + way = motorway

book + shelf = bookshelf

fire + work = firework

snow + man = snowman

Activities

1. Copy the two lists and draw lines to join words together, making compound words.

tooth	fish
rain	glasses
sun	brush
jelly	coat

2. Make a compound word by adding another word at the end.

   a. moon　　b. wheel　　c. tea　　d. bed

> **✓ Tip**
> To make a compound word easier to spell, split it into the words that make it up.

> **Key words**
> compound words

Curriculum objectives

- To form nouns by compounding. (Grammar appendix)

Success criteria

- I can join two nouns to make a new word.

100 English Lessons Year 2 links:

- Starter activity 7 (page 12): Join together
- Starter activity 16 (page 15): Knowing terminology

Year 2 Practice Book links:

- (page 60): Joined up
- (page 65): Take your partner
- (page 66): Picture sums

Words that sound the same and More words that sound the same

Prior learning

- Can read words with unusual graphemes.
- Understand homophones in context.

Learn

- Help children distinguish between 'its', the possessive pronoun, and 'it's', the contracted form of 'it is'. Remind the children about contractions. Ask them to explain what the apostrophe stands for in a contracted word. Write 'it's' on the board and ask them to tell you what is missing. Ask them to use 'it's' in a sentence.

- Now show them 'its', explaining that it indicates that something belongs to something or someone ('The dog eats its food.' The food belongs to the dog.) Write some examples of sentences using 'it's' and 'its' on the board with a line where 'it's' or 'its' should be. Tell the children that a good test for when to use 'it's' or 'its' is to replace them with 'it is' in the sentence ('The dog

Curriculum objectives

- To learn new ways of spelling phonemes for which one or more spellings are already known, and learn some words with each spelling, including a few common homophones.
- To distinguish between homophones and near-homophones.

Success criteria

- I can use 'its' and 'their' to show possession.
- I understand that some words sound the same but have different meanings.
- I can spell words that sound the same but are spelled differently and have different meanings.

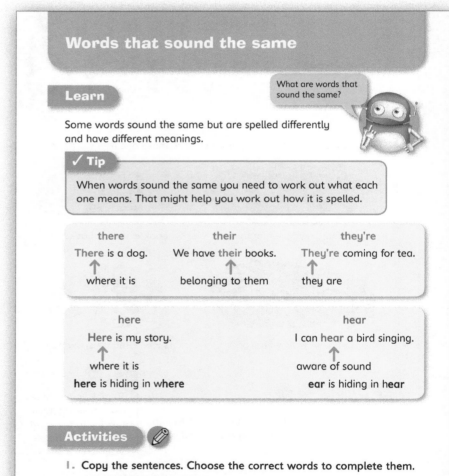

Words that sound the same

Learn

What are words that sound the same?

Some words sound the same but are spelled differently and have different meanings.

✓ Tip

When words sound the same you need to work out what each one means. That might help you work out how it is spelled.

there	their	they're
There is a dog.	We have their books.	They're coming for tea.
↑	↑	↑
where it is	belonging to them	they are

here	hear
Here is my story.	I can hear a bird singing.
↑	↑
where it is	aware of sound
here is hiding in where	ear is hiding in hear

Activities

1. **Copy the sentences. Choose the correct words to complete them.**

there	they're	their

   a. Look over ____!

   b. Have you wrapped ____ presents?

   c. I don't know if ____ here yet.

eats it is food.'). If the sentence makes sense, use 'it's', and if it doesn't, use 'its'.

- Another common homophone problem is 'there', 'they're' and 'their'. Children can use the same techniques to distinguish 'they're' and 'their'. Write the word 'there'. Can the children find the word 'here' within the word? Remind them that 'there' tells us about place. Write the word 'there' with

'here' in another colour. Note you can also use these techniques with the words 'we're', 'where' and 'wear'.

- Collect homophones from the texts you read. Make posters with pictures and sentences using the homophones in context to help children understand their meanings.

Activities

- Use the photocopiable sheet in *100 English Lessons Year 2* (page 200) 'Pirate story spellings' to investigate more homophones in context.

- Play games such as 'homophone snap' and use activities in the *Year 2 Practice Book* to get to know a variety of homophones.

- 'Its' and 'it's' are frequently confused, even by adults. Ask children to write 'its' and 'it's' on either side of their whiteboards. Write or say sentences containing 'its' and 'it's' and ask them to show you which version to use. Do this regularly so that the understanding becomes embedded.

More words that sound the same

Learn

its
The spider is in its web
↑
belonging to it

it's
It's a spider!
↑
short for **it is**

wear
You must wear gloves.
↑
put on

where
Where did you put your gloves?
↑
question word about position

ate
I ate a large pizza.
↑
had food

eight
A spider has eight legs.
↑
a number

Activities

1. **Write each sentence. Choose the correct bold word in each sentence.**

   a. There is a **sale / sail** on in our local bike shop.

   b. Jack went to **meat / meet** his friend.

   c. The dog hurt his **poor / pore / paw**.

2. **Write a sentence using each word.**

   a. sun   b. son

Spelling   51

100 English Lessons Year 2 links:

- Spring 1, Week 6 (page 99): Lesson 2, Homophone detectives

- Summer 2, Week 3 (page 186): Lesson 3, Helpful homophones

- Summer 2, Week 6 (pages 194–196): understand the difference between 'its' and 'it's'

Year 2 Practice Book links:

- (page 48): Snap!
- (page 49): Sounds like...
- (page 50): Pick the word
- (page 51): In the garden

Plurals with 's' and 'es'

Prior learning

- Know how to make a noun into a plural by adding 's'.
- Know how to add 's' to verbs.
- Terminology: noun, verb, plural, vowel, consonant.

Learn

- To make a noun that ends in 's', 'ss', 'ch', 'sh', 'zz' and 'x' plural, you add 'es'.
- Investigate which nouns take the ending 'es'. Give the children a variety of plural nouns including those with this ending. Ask them to sort the words by their endings. Can they identify why some words take the ending 'es'? Tell them that words that hiss ('ss', 's'), buzz ('x', 'zz') and shush ('sh', 'ch') all need 'es' at the end when they are plurals. Can they think of other words like this? Write a list of new hissing, buzzing and shushing words and investigate whether they take 's' or 'es' in the plural form.
- Nouns that end in a consonant and then 'y' follow the swap rule: swap the 'y' for an 'i' and add 'es'. However, words with the long vowel sound that end in 'ey', 'oy', 'ay' and 'uy' just take 's'. Makes lists of these two types of words in their plural forms. Can the children work out the root words and then make a rule for how to change them into plurals?
- Verbs in the simple present tense need to have 's' added to them in the third person ('she'/'he'/'it'). These verbs follow the same rules as the nouns. Verbs that hiss, buzz and shush need 'es'. Verbs ending in a consonant and then 'y' follow the swap rule. Swap the 'y' for an 'i' and add 'es'.) Create a short piece of writing in the first person and then model changing it into the third person to show children how the verbs change form. Give children short extracts to change.

Curriculum objectives

- To add 'es' to nouns and verbs ending in 'y'. (Spelling appendix)

Success criteria

- I know when to add 'es' to a noun to make it into a plural.
- I know that I swap the 'y' for an 'i' when I add 'es' to verbs ending in 'y'.

Plurals with 's' and 'es'

Learn

What is a plural?

A plural is when there is more than one of something.

For most singular words, just add s to make them plural.

Singular	Plural
a hat	several hats

Some singular words end in **x**, **ch**, **sh**, **s**, **ss** or **z**. Add **es** to make these words plural.

Singular	Plural
the box	many boxes
one beach	several beaches
a wish	three wishes

Some singular words end in **y**. To make these words plural, change y to i and add es.

Singular	Plural
one fairy	two fairies
a baby	many babies
the family	some families

If a word ends in **ay**, **ey**, **iy**, **oy** or **uy**, just add **s**.

Singular	Plural
one boy	two boys
a donkey	three donkeys
the toy	many toys

✓ **Tip**

If it sounds like s or z at the end, it ends in s.
If it sounds like iz at the end, it ends in es.

Key words

plural
singular

52   Spelling

- The textbook explores the rules for adding 'es' to nouns. Children find out how to choose between 's' and 'es' endings when making plurals. They consolidate this by choosing the correct spelling of plurals and writing plural words in sentences.

- Support children by showing them how to highlight the final sound in each word and decide if it hisses, buzzes or shushes, or if it ends in consonant 'y' before they choose to add 's' or 'es'.

- Make sound poems with the plural words that hiss, buzz and shush. Start off by listing the words, without the plurals, on sticky notes. Get the children to help you organise them so that you create a sound poem (it doesn't have to make sense, just create sounds), using alliteration and rhythm as well. Then change the words into plurals. How does that affect the poem? Do you want to change the words around? What does the poem sound like: the sea, the wind or something else?

Activities

1. Copy the table and write the singular or plural of these words.

Singular	Plural
window	
kiss	
	churches
	flowers
	toes

2. Write the plural of each word.

   a. tray

   b. lady

   c. lorry

   d. key

   e. fly

   f. berry

3. Write the plural of each word in brackets to complete the sentences.

   a. Lots of _____ (turkey) are sold at Christmas.

   b. We walked through several _____ (valley) before reaching the village.

   c. Some _____ (country) are often hot.

4. Write the correct plural from each pair of words.

   a. citys   cities

   b. butterflys   butterflies

   c. familys   families

   d. monkeys   monkeies

5. Look at the above words. What is the rule for making the plural of a word ending in 'y'?

   Is there a vowel before y? Just add **s**. If there is no vowel before y, change y to **i** and add **es**.

Year 2 Practice Book links:

- (page 16): Drop the 'y', add the 'i' (1)
- (page 17): New endings
- (page 18): Find the letter

Ordering events and Explaining the order of events

Prior learning

- Sequence simple, familiar events (the school day, eating breakfast).
- Understand that stories are made up of a series of events.

- Understanding the sequencing of events is crucial in developing good comprehension. When reading a story, children need to be able to work out who are the main characters and what are the main events. Initially, children will need support in this, but they will grow in independence over time.

- Use the activities in *100 English Lessons Year 2* such as sequencing mixed-up sentences, retelling stories using story maps and acting out stories to help children's confidence.

Learn

- Start off by talking about common events in children's lives such as getting ready for school, eating breakfast and getting dressed. Use pictures or get the children to act out these events. Break up the sequence of events so children can see each part. Come up with a caption for each part of the sequence, such as 'get a bowl and spoon', 'put them on the table', or similar. Ask the children to tell you the sequence of events. Write the sequence out of order: can the children work out what the order should be? Give them the sentences cut up into strips. Can they put them into the correct order?

Curriculum objectives

- To discuss the sequence of events in books and how items of information are related.
- To participate in discussion about books, poems and other works that are read to them and those that they can read for themselves, taking turns and listening to what others say.

Success criteria

- I can arrange sentences from a story into the correct sequence.
- I can retell a story using a story map.

Ordering events

Learn

What does ordering events mean?

Events are things that happen in a piece of writing. You need to be able to find events and put them in the order that they happen.

> **Ralf's first day**
>
> It was Ralf's first day at school. He walked up the drive with his mother. As soon as they started to cross the playground, Ralf saw lots of bigger boys and girls.

← 1st event

← 2nd event
← 3rd event

Here are the events in order:
1. He walked up the drive with his mother.
2. They started to cross the playground.
3. Ralf saw lots of bigger boys and girls.

Activities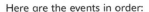

1. **Read the next part of Ralf's story.**

> Some of the children started running around near him. It became very noisy. Ralf held his mother's hand tightly. As the teacher met them at the door, she was smiling. She looked friendly. Ralf thought that everything would be all right.

Read the events below and write them in the correct order.

The teacher met them at the door.

Ralf held his mother's hand tightly.

Some of the children started running around near Ralf.

Use story maps such as those in *100 English Lessons Year 2* and on the CD-ROM as the basis of retelling a well-known story as a class. Use actions to help children remember the key parts of the sequence (act out verbs, use hand gestures to show adverbial language such as 'next'). Encourage children to refer to the story map as they retell the story. When they are confident at retelling the story, ask them to think about other stories that have similar events. How are they similar/different? Encourage them to share their views and build on what the previous child has said.

- Use the textbook to help children sequence events. Children consider how each part of the sequence of events is connected.
- Some children will need to start by sequencing simple, familiar events, such as eating breakfast or dressing, before they sequence the events from a story. Use picture-sequencing cards initially and move on to story maps to ensure these children are successful at each stage.
- There are several activities in *100 English Lessons Year 2* and on the CD-ROM including sentence sequencing activities and story maps.

Explaining the order of events

Learn

What does it mean to explain the order of events?

When you explain the order of events, you say why things happened in the order they did.

In this story, the events are numbered for you.

Juggling

(1) My dad bought my sister, Anna, some juggling balls and a book on how to juggle for her sixth birthday.
(2) By the time she was seven she had given up using them. It was far too hard. **(3)** For Anna's next birthday, Dad gave her a DVD on how to juggle. That made it much easier.

Explain why Anna's dad bought her a DVD for her seventh birthday.

This question is about the 3rd event. Look at the 1st and 2nd events to work out the answer.

Anna's dad bought her a DVD because she had tried using a book but it was too hard so she had given up.

Activities

1. Read the next part of the story.

Soon Anna could juggle with three balls. It took her another year to be able to do it with four. By then it was easy, so she tried with much more difficult things like bottles and cups. She had to stop using the cups, as she broke so many we didn't have enough left to drink from!

Why did Anna use bottles and cups after the juggling balls?

Reading **55**

100 English Lessons Year 2 links:

How texts are organised

Prior learning

- Know the difference between fiction and non-fiction.

Learn

- Make sure that the children understand the purpose of non-fiction books by asking them why they might choose to read one. Choose a book and ask the children to tell you how they would look for specific information within it. Explain how the contents page and index are the first places to look.

- Ask children to look at how different non-fiction books are organised and make a list of organisational features together. Go through the list and discuss how these features help the reader.

Curriculum objectives

- To discuss how items of information are related.
- To be introduced to non-fiction books structured in different ways.

Success criteria

- I can discuss the sequence of events in a book.
- I can talk about how information is organised in a non-fiction book.
- I can use headings, tables and other features to help me find information in a non-fiction book.

How texts are organised

How are texts organised?

Learn

Texts can be organised in many different ways. Writers organise their texts to make them easier to read.

Ways of organising texts include headings, subheadings, numbers and bullet points.

heading: tells you what the whole piece of writing is about

The Moon

People have watched the Moon since the beginning of time. Many people have dreamed of going there, but only a few have been.

Walking on the Moon
The first person to walk on the Moon was Neil Armstrong in 1969. He landed there with Buzz Aldrin. The last person walked on the moon in December 1972. No one has been there since.

subheading: tells you the particular thing this part of the writing is about

heading: tells you what the whole piece of writing is about

Boiling water in a kettle
1. Put enough water in the kettle.
2. Plug the kettle in.
3. Switch the kettle on.
4. Wait for the water to boil.

numbers: tell you the order things are done

- Talk to the children about the purpose of different types of non-fiction texts. Ask them if the purpose of the text makes a difference to how it is organised. Use recipes and leaflets as examples.

- For more coverage of sequencing stories and events see 'Ordering events' and 'Explaining the order of events' on pages 58–59 of this book.

- The textbook explains the main features of non-fiction books. It gives clear examples of headings, subheadings, numbered instructions and bullet points, and it explains the purpose of these features. You can expand the list of features of non-fiction books by including fact boxes, captions, illustrations, pictures/photographs, questions, indexes, contents page and introductions.

- There are examples of non-fiction texts in *100 English Lessons Year 2* as well as an interactive activity to sort features of fiction and non-fiction texts on the CD-ROM.

Shopping list

- 3 onions
- A litre of milk
- Teabags
- Flowers

heading: tells you what the whole piece of writing is about

bullet points: tell you what is needed, but not the order

Activities

1. In *The Moon*, what ways are used to organise the text? **Write two.**

   headings   bullet points   numbers   subheadings

2. Look at the lists below. Match each way of organising a text to what it tells you and write them down.

Way of organising a text	What it tells you
headings	the order things are done
subheadings	what the whole piece of writing is about
numbers	what is needed, but not the order
bullet points	what a part of the writing is about

3. Which text uses bullet points?

4. Look at *Boiling water in a kettle*. Why does this text have numbers rather than bullet points?

100 English Lessons Year 2 links:

- Autumn 1, Week 3 (page 26): Lesson 2, What's in a recipe?
- Autumn 2, Week 4 (page 60): Lesson 1, Instructions recap
- Spring 1, Week 4 (page 94): Lesson 4, Writing a factfile (1)
- Spring 2, Week 3 (page 123): Lesson 4, Non-fiction report
- Spring 2, Assess and review (page 134): Comparing fiction and non-fiction
- Summer 1, Week 3 (page 154): Lesson 2, Reading leaflets
- Summer 2, Week 2 (page 182): Lesson 1, Pirate life

Year 2 Practice Book links:

- (pages 100–101): Finding out from charts
- (pages 104–105): Making a pancake
- (pages 116–117): Dinosaur facts

What words mean

Prior learning

- Can decode words with unusual graphemes.
- Can segment longer words when reading.

Learn

- Before reading, identify the new vocabulary and explain meanings to the children. Ask them to look out for the words in the story. After reading, return to the new vocabulary and check understanding.

- Ask the children to keep a record of words they don't understand. Create a class word list with definitions and examples. Encourage the children to use these new words in class.

- Teach the children how root words can be extended with suffixes and prefixes. Choose an unusual word such as 'enlightened' and help them strip it back to its root 'en-light-en-ed'. Use the children's knowledge of

root words and suffixes to work out what the original word means. Can the children do this with other words?

- Create banks of synonymous language: alternatives for common words such as 'nice', 'good', 'sad', 'happy'. Practise using these words in different contexts, for example, use synonymous words to replace words in a text. Does the meaning of the sentence remain or subtly change?

Talk

- Use synonymous language to extend the children's vocabulary. Use the word banks that you made with the children as the basis for some games. Play 'I'm not just…': say to the children *'I'm not just happy, I'm delighted.'* Can they use another word from the 'happy' word bank to show you are even more than

Curriculum objectives

- To discuss and clarify the meanings of words, linking new meanings to known vocabulary.
- To draw on what they already know or on background information and vocabulary provided by the teacher.

Success criteria

- I can decode new words.
- I can use information from the sentence to help me work out a new word.
- I can use what I already know to work out what a new word means.

What words mean

> How do we know what words mean?

Learn

Sometimes when you are reading, you come across a word you don't understand. You can use what you know already to work out what the word means.

Last night's firework display was an electrifying event that thrilled thousands of people.

What does **electrifying** mean in this sentence?

Read the whole sentence and look for clues.

| Last night's firework **display** was an **electrifying** event that **thrilled** thousands of people. | unknown word clues |

Use the clues to help you work out what the unknown word means.

A **display** is something you watch or look at.
Thrilled means excited.
So in this sentence, **electrifying** might mean *exciting to watch.*

Another way to work out what the word means is to see if it looks like a word you already know.

Electrifying looks like **electric** or **electricity**. Electricity is used for lights. It can cause large sparks. In this sentence electrifying might mean having lots of bright lights or sparks.

> So, in this piece of writing, electrifying means exciting to watch or full of bright lights.

delighted? Keep going for as long as you can! Do the same with 'I'm not just sad, I'm glum', 'The present is not just nice, its great', 'The witch is not just bad, she's dreadful.'

- Play opposites with the children. See if they can find more than one word that is the opposite of 'happy', 'sad', 'naughty', 'good', 'fast', and so on.

- The textbook shows children how to use context clues and the root of a new word to work out its meaning. They can consolidate their skills by working out the meanings of words in the activities.

- Poems are a good medium to explore the meaning of words and there are several that you can use on the *100 English Lessons Year 2* CD-ROM.

- The *Year 2 Practice Book* and *100 English Lessons Year 2* contain activities where children choose the correct word to complete sentences. This will consolidate their understanding of homophones and new vocabulary.

Activities

1. The wind blew fiercely across the field.

   Which word tells us that the wind was blowing very strongly?

2. Leaves were shredded from the trees.

   In this sentence, 'shredded' means:
   taken   hanging   ripped   floating

3. Suddenly, the storm stopped as briskly as it had started.

   What does the word 'briskly' mean in this sentence?

> ✓ Tip
>
> If you don't know what a word means, read the whole sentence and see if you can work it out.

Reading **59**

100 English Lessons Year 2 links:

- Autumn 1, Week 6 (page 34): Lesson 1, Spaghetti
- Autumn 2, Week 1 (pages 51–53): decode and discuss the meaning of new vocabulary
- Autumn 2, Week 2 (pages 54–56): discuss the meaning of new vocabulary found in fairy-tale settings
- Autumn 2, Week 6 (page 66): Lesson 1, One, two, buckle my shoe
- Summer 2, Week 1 (page 180): Lesson 2, Features of pirate stories
- Summer 2, Week 4 (page 188): Lesson 1, *Treasure Island*

Year 2 Practice Book links:

- (page 62): Superhero or not?
- (pages 108–109): Painting

Explaining characters and events

Prior learning

- Can identify what characters are feeling.
- Can sequence events in a story.

Learn

- Use a familiar story like 'Little Red Riding Hood' to illustrate cause and effect.

Curriculum objectives

- To explain and discuss their understanding of books, poems and other material, both those that they listen to and those that they read for themselves.

Success criteria

- I can give reasons about why a character feels something.
- I can find the reason behind an event occurring.

100 English Lessons Year 2 links:

- Autumn 2, Week 2 (page 55): Lesson 2, Setting role play
- Spring 1, Week 1 (page 85): Lesson 5, Question time
- Spring 2, Week 1 (page 116): Lesson 3, Questions, questions
- Spring 2, Week 4 (page 126): Lesson 4, Game cards
- Summer 1, Week 4 (page 156–158): explore differences between two characters

Year 2 Practice Book links:

- (pages 106–107): The tortoises
- (pages 112–113): Missing mouse
- (pages 114–115): Noses

- Write 'Cause' and 'Effect' on the board. Write the events of the story under these headings.
- Ask children for events that have affected their behaviour, such as 'When my brother got a toy and I didn't, I felt upset so I sulked.'
- Explore how characters' feelings are rooted in what happens to them.
- Use 'why' and 'how' questions to uncover the reasons behind events and characters' behaviour.

Activities

- The textbook examples show how to find the reasons behind events and characters' actions and feelings.
- Encourage children to give reasons for their inferences when you explore characters' feelings and behaviour. Many activities in *100 English Lessons Year 2* use this approach.

Explaining characters and events

Learn

What does it mean to explain characters and events?

Explain means to say **why** or **how**. You have to give **reasons**.

Characters: You have to be able to explain what characters are like or why they do things.

Adele was angry. She had lost her phone

↑   ↑
what Adele **is like**   the **reason** why

Events: You have to be able to explain why something happened.

event → Dad checked the petrol in the car. It was
reason → nearly empty, so he went to the garage ← event
to fill it up.

The **reason** explains why the second event happened.

Activities

1. Nasreen is very funny. She makes everyone laugh. We are all happy when Nasreen is here.

    Why does everyone like Nasreen?

2. Amina always went to the supermarket on Sunday mornings because it was quiet.

    Why did Amina always go to the supermarket on Sunday mornings?

Explaining information

Prior learning

- Can read non-fiction to retrieve information.

Learn

- To explain non-fiction, children need to be able to find out why and how something happens.
- Choose simple information texts and ask 'how' and 'why' questions to uncover the reasons for facts and events. Show children how you take the information from the text to help you write an answer.
- Model composing answers to 'how' and 'why' questions by using subordinating conjunctions such as 'because', 'this is because' and 'so that'.

Activities

- The textbook has clear examples of how to make an explanation by asking 'how' and 'why' questions.
- Use the *Year 2 Practice Book* to explore non-fiction texts.

- Encourage children to think carefully about the main message when they read non-fiction.

Write

- Encourage children to write 'how' and 'why' questions about non-fiction texts for other children to answer.

Curriculum objectives

- To explain and discuss their understanding of books, poems and other material, both those that they listen to and those that they read for themselves.

Success criteria

- I can find out why things happen in non-fiction.
- I can find information that explains how things happen in non-fiction.

Explaining information

Learn

What does it mean to explain information?

Explain means to say **why** or **how**. You have to give **reasons**.

You have to be able to explain the reason for a piece of information.

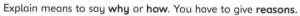

In the Arctic, the ice is melting. This means polar bears are in danger.

reason   information

Why are the polar bears in danger?
Because the ice is melting.

Activities

1. Tigers are good at hunting. They can run fast and have sharp claws and teeth.

Why are tigers good at hunting?

✓ Tip

When you explain, first think **Why?** or **How?** and then give a **reason**.

Reading **61**

100 English Lessons Year 2 links:

- Autumn 1, Week 4 (page 28): Lesson 1, Creating a new recipe
- Autumn 2, Week 4 (page 61) Lesson 2, Improving poor instructions
- Spring 2, Week 1 (page 116): Lesson 3, Questions, questions
- Spring 2, Week 4 (page 126): Lesson 4, Game cards
- Summer 1, Week 3 (pages 153–155): find links between habitats and resident animals

Year 2 Practice Book links:

- (pages 100–101): Finding out from charts

Predicting what might happen

Prior learning

- Terminology: plot, character, setting
- Can draw out common themes, plot types and characters.

Learn

- Ask children to tell you about typical features of stories they know well, such as fairy tales, adventures or school-based stories. Draw out predictable story patterns: there is a problem that has to be solved, someone wishes for something, and so on. Ask children to think about how different types of characters behave: the hero is brave and kind, the baddies are sneaky and mean. Can they make predictions about how some stories typically end? Collect all this information and show the class how much they know about how stories work. Using all this knowledge helps them understand stories and enjoy them even more.

Curriculum objectives

- To predict what might happen on the basis of what has been read so far.
- To explain and discuss their understanding of books, poems and other material, both those that they listen to and those that they read for themselves.

Success criteria

- I can make a prediction based on the events in the story so far.
- I can make a prediction based on my knowledge of stories and characters.

- Write some short descriptions of settings on the board such as the dark, dark wood; the edge of a cliff; an empty school; a palace ballroom; a treasure island. Ask the children to discuss what sort of stories the settings belong to and what events they expect to take place in the different settings.

- Help children make predictions when they begin reading a story. Show them what you think when you look at the cover and title of the book. Read the first page and tell them about the connections to other stories you have made, and how that helps you imagine the book you are about to read.

Predicting what might happen

How do you predict what might happen?

Learn

Predicting is where you **guess** what will take place next. You use what you have read to help you guess.

To predict, you need to read the whole text and then say what might happen next. In this text, the clues have been highlighted.

> Sam looked at the clock. **Only three minutes** to catch the bus! He put his coat on, but **it took him a long time to do the zip.** When he went out, **the key wouldn't work** to lock the door. He ran down the street but **tripped up and fell on the floor.**

Sam is trying to catch the bus. Do you think he will make it?

Clues	What the clues tell us
He only had three minutes. →	He hasn't got long to catch the bus.
His zip took a long time. →	The zip slows him down.
The key wouldn't work. →	The key slows him down more.
He fell on the floor. →	Falling over will slow him down even more.

The clues tell us: Sam is not likely to catch the bus because he will run out of time.

Activities

1. **Write down the clues in this text that tell you what might happen next.**

> Lorna was going very fast on her bike. She needed to stop quickly. She pulled hard on her brakes. There was a loud snap and her front brake fell off!

Activities

Tell them about the questions you ask yourself as you read, and the predictions you make. Ask the children to choose a book and do the same thing. Write prompts on the board such as 'What do the cover and title make me think about?', 'Which other books does this one remind me of?', 'What characters do I know that are like these characters?', 'Are there any questions I want answered?', 'What do I expect to happen next?'

- The textbook explains how we make predictions using the clues in the text. There are several activities that help children increase their confidence at making predictions.

- Use the activity in the *Year 2 Practice Book* for children to make independent predictions about a story.

- Support children who find this tricky by making wildly implausible predictions about stories and getting them to explain why they are so unlikely. By doing so, they will use their knowledge of the story and be closer to making their own prediction.

2. **What do you think might happen next? It seems like she will crash but she might not. Make a list of all of the things that you think could take place after her brake falls off.**

3. **From your list, pick the two things you think are most likely to happen. Give a reason for each one.**

4. **This is the next part of Lorna's story. Did you predict it?**

> Lorna shot across the road. A car was coming in her direction! The car driver pressed his brake pedal as hard as he could and closed his eyes. Lorna closed her eyes too. When she opened them she could hear the sound of an ambulance.

5. **To predict what happens next, you have to work out what has just happened. The ambulance is coming for a reason. Someone must be hurt. Write down three possible things that could happen next. Give a reason for each one.**

6. **This is not the end of Lorna's story. Make a list of the other people that might come into the story. What do you think they might do?**

7. **What do you think will happen at the end of the story? Give a reason for your thoughts.**

8. **Share your ideas about the ending with a partner. Talk about what might happen and why. What do you both think is the best idea? Now work together to write the ending of Lorna's story.**

Reading **63**

100 English Lessons Year 2 links:

- Autumn 1, Week 1 (page 19): Lesson 1, *Oliver's Vegetables*
- Autumn 1, Assess and review (page 38): Predicting events
- Spring 1, Week 1 (page 84): Lesson 2, Introducing *Zoo*
- Spring 2, Week 1 (page 115): Lesson 1, Introducing *Funnybones*
- Summer 1, Week 4 (page 156): Lesson 1, Welcome to Struay
- Summer 2, Week 4 (page 188): Lesson 1, *Treasure Island*

Year 2 Practice Book links:

- (pages 112–113) Missing Mouse

Making inferences

Prior learning

- Can learn about characters from what they say and do.

Learn

- Making inferences is a key skill that readers use to bring a story alive. Model how you make inferences by 'thinking out loud' as you read a short section of a story. Tell the children how you pick up clues in the text to explain why events happen or why characters behave as they do. Explain that your inferences are based on the story, your experiences of other stories and your life. Also explain that for you to fully enjoy the story, your inferences have to make sense: they can't be implausible.

- Point out the words and phrases in the text that give you the clues on which you are basing your inferences. Ask the children to infer how a character is feeling and tell them to identify the clues they have found as a basis for their inferences.

- Act in role as a character from a familiar story such as 'Little Red Riding Hood'. Retell the story from the character's point of view, giving your opinion about characters, events and other information that is not in the story, and include one implausible event/opinion. Ask the children to discuss which parts of your story were in the original and which parts you inferred. Can they work out where in the story you got your inferences? Did anything seem out of place?

Curriculum objectives

- To make inferences on the basis of what is being said and done.
- To draw on what they already know or on background information and vocabulary provided by the teacher.

Success criteria

- I can make inferences based on what characters say and do.
- I can make inferences based on clues in the text.
- I can empathise with a character.
- I can act in role and infer how a character might feel.

Making inferences

Learn

How do you make inferences?

When you make inferences you work out what has happened. You give a reason **why** you think it has happened.

> Ethan put his hand in his pocket to get the money to pay for his sweets. There was nothing there! He had put a pound coin in his pocket before he left home, but it wasn't there any more.

We know what has happened. Ethan had a pound coin in his pocket but he doesn't have it any more.
We don't know **why** he doesn't have it, so we have to guess.

The pound coin could:

- have fallen out of Ethan's pocket.
- have fallen through a hole in the pocket.
- have been stolen.
- still be there but Ethan just can't find it.
- have gone through a hole in the pocket and be stuck in the lining.

We don't know!

✓ Tip

Look for reasons why something might have happened.

- The activities in the textbook explain how you can make inferences from the clues in a text and also support children in finding clues in texts before they make an inference.

- Support children who find this activity difficult by using a grid such as *100 English Lessons Year 2* (page 104) 'Actions and moods' to make links between how a character behaves and how they might feel.

- The *Year 2 Practice Book* comprehension activities require simple inference.

Activities

1. **Read the next part of Ethan's story.**

   > Ethan felt in his pocket again and was surprised when his finger went all the way through and out of the other side.

   a. What do you think has happened to the pound coin?

   b. Why do you think it happened?

2. **Which word tells us that Ashran has not had much to eat?**

   > Ashran looked hungrily at the cakes in the shop window.

3. **Which word shows what the captain is like?**

   > The captain bravely saved the young girl from the water.

4. **Read this short story.**

   > Georgia sprang out of bed and ran downstairs. She did not usually do this but today was her birthday! She jumped up and down for joy. There on the table was her present. She felt it carefully then tore open the paper. It was just what she wanted!

   How do you think Georgia is feeling? Give two reasons for your answer.

   > ✓ **Tip**
   >
   > Sometimes when we make inferences, we work out what someone is like or how they are feeling.

100 English Lessons Year 2 links:

Year 2 Practice Book links:

Talking about texts

Prior learning

- Can use phonic knowledge to decode and blend new words.
- Can read phonically decodable words with fluency.
- Can draw on what is already known about stories and on background information and vocabulary.

Learn

- An important facet to being a reader is your personal response to a book. Sometimes we are delighted or annoyed by a twist of a story, or the way a character behaves, or the way a phrase is constructed. Develop this in children by talking to them about what you enjoy in books that you read with them. Tell them about your reactions to characters and events in the story.

Curriculum objectives

- To discuss their favourite words and phrases.
- To check that the text makes sense to them as they read and to correct inaccurate reading.

Success criteria

- I can talk about my favourite words and phrases and say why I like them.
- I can link what I read to what I already know.
- I can check that I understand what I read.
- I can decode new words.
- I can ask questions to explore a text.

- After reading, ask the children to discuss whichever part of the text stood out for them. Draw out why it was especially vivid for them by asking questions such as 'Did it remind you of something you have read or experienced?', 'Have you read anything like that before?', 'Did that surprise you? Why?', 'What does that look like in your mind?'

- Sometimes we are confused or intrigued by what we read; we like it but we aren't sure why. Help children understand imagery in texts by ensuring that they understand the meaning of the words (these often change slightly because of the context).

Talking about texts

How do you talk about what you have read?

Learn

When you talk about a text:
- You **say what you like** about it.
- You **find out what words mean**.
- You check that the **writing makes sense** to you.
- You **ask and answer questions** about what you have read.

In this poem, the writer helps you to see what is happening by the way he describes it:

> The Owl and the Pussycat went to sea
> In a beautiful pea green boat,
> They took some honey, and plenty of money,
> Wrapped up in a five pound note
>
> From the *Owl and the Pussycat* by Edward Lear

What you might like

If you were asked what you liked about the poem, you might say:
"*In a beautiful pea green boat* tells us exactly what colour the boat was. The poem is made more interesting by the use of **rhyme** – money and honey, boat and note. I liked the idea of the owl and the pussycat taking a five pound note. What would they use it for?"

What do the words mean?

Most of the words in the poem are not difficult to understand. *Wrapped* might be strange to you. The silent w makes it hard to read. If you're not sure what a word means, look it up in a dictionary.

Does it make sense?

You might think that the poem doesn't make sense at all. If so, you might be right! Edward Lear wrote what he called 'nonsense poems' – they weren't meant to make sense! If it's not clear, you will have to ask some questions.

- Encourage children to enjoy the writer's choice of words and phrases. Keep a wall of words and phrases that the children have told you they find arresting. They may want to 'borrow' some of them as they write.

Activities

- The *Year 2 Practice Book* outlines a strategy to help children talk about what they have read. They can practise this strategy in the activities.
- There is ample support in *100 English Lessons Year 2* to ensure children talk about the language in books and develop an interest in how writers use words to create vivid images.

Write

- Make a big book in which the children can write their opinions and ideas about stories, poems and non-fiction. Encourage them to write about language they enjoy or particular characters they feel strongly about. They could respond to the illustrations or an event that they were delighted or surprised by. This book should not be a collection of reviews, but rather a collection of personal responses.

Any questions?

There are a lot of things in the poem that might not happen:

- Would a cat and an owl sail a boat?
- Would they need money?
- Can you wrap honey up?

If you talk about them, they might make sense.

Activities

I. **Read this poem.**

a. What do the following words mean in the poem?

| stalk | hovering |

Use a dictionary if you are not sure.

b. With a partner, talk about what *No toad spy you* means.

c. With a partner, talk about what you like about the poem.

d. With a partner, talk about the ending. How can the caterpillar die and live again?

e. Make a list of questions you might like to ask your teacher about the poem.

Caterpillar

Brown and furry
Caterpillar in a hurry,
Take your walk
To the shady leaf, or stalk,
Or what not,
Which may be the chosen spot.
No toad spy you,
Hovering bird of prey pass by you;
Spin and die,
To live again a butterfly.

Christina Rossetti

Reading **67**

100 English Lessons Year 2 links:

- Autumn 1, Week 1 (page 19): Lesson 1, *Oliver's Vegetables*
- Spring 1, Week 1 (page 84): Lesson 2, Introducing *Zoo*
- Spring 1, Week 6 (page 98): Lesson 1, Zoo poems
- Spring 2, Week 6 (page 130): Lesson 1, Poetry about the senses
- Summer 1, Week 2 (page 150): Lesson 1, Snow in the suburbs
- Summer 1, Assess and review (page 166): Sequencing stories
- Summer 2, Week 1 (page 179): Lesson 1, Discovering pirates
- Summer 2, Week 5 (page 191): Lesson 1, Words to treasure

Looking at language in stories and poetry

Prior learning

- Are familiar with nursery rhymes.
- Can make an opinion about what they have read.

Learn

- Read poems aloud to the children with intonation so they can hear the rhythm and rhyme. Ask them to discuss the words and phrases they enjoyed. Draw out why they enjoyed them.

- Read a poem that has a simple rhyming pattern. Ask the children to tell you which words rhyme. Explore the spelling of the rhyming words: do they always follow the same spelling pattern?

- Poems don't have to rhyme, but many poems do. Read some poems that don't rhyme and ask the children what they think of them. Explain that the rhythm of the poem is just as important, and explore this by counting out the beats. Does it still seem like a poem? Why? Show the children how the poem is structured on the page: do they think this is important?

Curriculum objectives

- To recognise simple recurring literary language in stories and poetry.

Success criteria

- I can recognise a poem.
- I can find words that rhyme in a poem.

Looking at language in stories and poetry

Learn

When you look at language in stories and poetry, look for rhymes and for words that are repeated.

What language should you look for?

Rhymes

These are words that sound like each other. They might not look like each other.

Word	Rhymes
could	would, wood, hood, should, stood
now	how, cow, bow, bough, row
sky	fly, try, sigh, sty, why

Key words

poetry
rhymes

Rhymes often appear in poetry.

In this poem, the rhymes come at the end of the lines:

> The Oak is called the king of trees,
> The Aspen quivers in the breeze,
> The Poplar grows up straight and tall,
> The Peach tree spreads along the wall.
>
> From *Trees* by Sara Coleridge

Each line is about a different tree – the Oak, the Aspen, the Poplar and the Peach.
Look at tall and wall. They look the same and rhyme.
Now look at trees and breeze. They rhyme, even though they don't look the same.

Some words are **repeated** in many stories. How many stories begin *Once upon a time*?

- Explore poems with specific syllable patterns, such as haiku.

- Show the children poems with alliteration and ask them to read these aloud. How does the repetition of a letter or sound make them feel? What effect do they think this repeated sound has?

- Ask children to think about why people write poems. How is a poem different to a story or a piece of non-fiction?

- Draw attention to repeated motifs in stories: the children will be familiar with ones from traditional tales such as 'I'll huff and I'll puff and I'll blow your house down', but these are also used in current literature. Why do they think the author uses repeated words and phrases?

Activities

- The textbook explores the use of rhyme and repetition in poetry and stories. Extend the activities by asking children to find other stories and poems with repeated words or rhymes.

- Collect words that describe elements of different types of stories and poems from the activities in *100 English Lessons Year 2* and create a class glossary of literary terms.

Activities

1. **Read this poem.**

   a. Make a list of the rhymes in this poem.

   b. Which two words should rhyme but don't quite?

   c. Why do you think the writer does not use another word to rhyme with orange?

What is pink?

What is pink? A rose is pink
By the fountain's brink.
What is red? A poppy's red
In its barley bed.
What is blue? The sky is blue
Where the clouds float through.
What is white? A swan is white
Sailing in the light.
What is yellow? Pears are yellow,
Rich and ripe and mellow.
What is green? The grass is green,
With small flowers between.
What is violet? Clouds are violet
In the summer twilight.
What is orange? Why, an orange,
Just an orange!

Christina Rossetti

2. **Read *The Gruffalo* by Julia Donaldson. What is repeated in it?**

3. **This poem repeats words and has rhymes. What is repeated? Which words rhyme?**

Kite

I didn't want to fly my kite,
I didn't want to try.
I didn't want it to fall from a height,
I didn't want to cry.

Graham Fletcher

100 English Lessons Year 2 links:

- Autumn 1, Week 2 (page 22): Lesson 1, Little Red Hen

- Autumn 2, Week 1 (page 52): Lesson 2, Once upon a time…

- Spring 2, Week 1 (page 116): Lesson 2, Sentence types

- Spring 2, Week 6 (page 130): Lesson 1, Poetry about the senses

Year 2 Practice Book links:

- (pages 102–103): Winter morning

Personal experiences and Fiction

Prior learning

- Can talk about things that matter to them such as family, pets and hobbies.
- Understand how to write in sentences.

Learn

- In Year 2, children are encouraged to write about what they know. They are more likely to be motivated to write about subjects that interest them or those they have experience of. Make a poll of activities that they enjoy doing at home or in clubs. Encourage them to bring in pictures or artefacts related to these activities.

Talk

- Tell the children that they are going to tell another child about something they enjoy doing at home. Give them questions to scaffold their talk. Give guidance about how to show their enthusiasm and enjoyment through the way they talk and the words they choose. Ask if any of them would like to share their talk with the class.

- Show the children how to turn the planning for their talk into a piece of writing. Remind them of how they organised their talk using keywords and answering questions. Tell the children to write their talk down by answering each question.

Curriculum objectives

- To write narratives about personal experiences and those of others (real and fictional).
- To plan or say out loud what they are going to write about.
- To write down ideas and/ or keywords, including new vocabulary.
- To encapsulate what they want to say, sentence by sentence.

Success criteria

- I can talk about a personal experience using a plan to help me.
- I can turn my talk into a piece of writing.

Personal experiences

> How do I write about personal experiences?

Learn

A personal experience is something that you know about or something that you have done. Choose a personal experience to write about, for example you could write about a pet.

Start by planning your writing – ask yourself some questions:

> What type of pet is it?

> What does it look like?

> What is its name?

> What can you do with your pet?

Make a note of your answers.

Non-fiction writing

> Every sentence starts with a capital letter and ends with a full stop.

My pet

My pet is a dog. She is a labrador and her name is Sandy. She loves long walks and getting muddy. When we get her lead out she becomes very excited because she knows she is going for a walk.

> Verb endings agree with doer.

> All sentences make sense and are written in the same tense.

Activities ✏️

1. **Write a non-fiction text about a pet. It could be your own or one you know. Decide what kind of animal it is. Plan your writing using the speech bubble questions to help you.**

   - Share ideas with a partner. Try and add more interesting details.
   - Now write your description of your pet. Remember to write in full sentences and check that it makes sense.

- The textbook gives an example of how to plan and write about a pet. These ideas and prompts could be used to plan writing other pieces of non-fiction. There is also support for planning fiction based on real experiences.

- You can use questions to help children scaffold their planning such as *100 English Lessons Year 2* (page 78) 'Diary questions' and (page 138) 'The five Ws'.

- You can use the activity in the *Year 2 Practice Book* to scaffold children's writing about personal experiences.

Write

- Ask children to keep a diary for a week. Explain that it is a personal record of their life and thoughts and you will not read it. After the time is up, ask the children to discuss what it is like writing about themselves every day. Will they continue? Show the children some extracts from famous diaries such as Roald Dahl's.

100 English Lessons Year 2 links:

- Autumn 2, Week 3 (pages 57–59): write a new fairy tale
- Autumn 2, Week 5 (pages 63–65): write a personal diary entry
- Spring 1, Week 2 (pages 86–88): plan a narrative based on characters' experiences
- Summer 1, Week 4 (pages 156–158): plan a recount based on the Katie Morag books
- Summer 1, Week 5 (pages 159–161): write biographies about characters they know well
- Summer 1, Week 6 (pages 162–164): write a story based on island life
- Summer 1, Assess and review (page 167): Writing about real events
- Summer 2, Week 2 (pages 182–184): write a ship's log based on drama
- Summer 2, Week 5 (pages 191–193): plan an adventure story

Year 2 Practice Book links:

- (page 118): My lunch box

Fiction

Learn

When you write about a topic you need to make a simple plan to help you organise your writing.

- Describe your pet
- What interesting/exciting things happen?
- How did you feel?
- How does it end?

> Sandy is a lively and friendly labrador. Usually she is very well behaved but one day she just wouldn't do as she was told. She dragged me into the woods and made me walk until we reached a small hut. When we found the hut, Sandy began barking loudly and wagged her tail enthusiastically. Did she want me to go in the hut? I was a bit frightened, but cautiously I turned the knob and went inside.

adjectives

starts the story

feelings

Activities

1. **You are going to write a story about an amazing or very naughty pet.**

   Think about:
   - How you will start your story or introduce your pet.
   - What naughty or amazing thing your pet will do.
   - How your adventure will end.

   Share your ideas with a partner. Remember to ask each other questions about the story. Now write your story.

✓ Tip

Your writing must make sense. Write in sentences. Make sure it is written in the same tense. Use interesting verbs, adjectives and adverbs.

Writing **71**

Real events

Prior learning

- Can talk about events in their lives.
- Understand that things that have happened are written about in the past tense.

Learn

- In Year 2, children are encouraged to write about their experiences. Children find it easier to write about things they have direct experience of, such as days out, birthdays, family events and school events.

Curriculum objectives

- To write about real events.
- To plan or say out loud what they are going to write about.
- To write down ideas and/ or keywords, including new vocabulary.
- To encapsulate what they want to say, sentence by sentence.

Success criteria

- I can write about things that have happened to me.

- Ask the children to think about a memorable event in their lives. What made it memorable? What details can they remember? Use *100 English Lessons Year 2* (page 138) 'The five Ws' to model writing down the details for an event all the children have experienced, such as doing class assembly.

- Next, ask the children to work in pairs to talk about their life event and fill out the same photocopiable sheet. Ensure they talk through each detail before they write it down.
- Show the children how you used your plan to help you write sentences that describe the event. Draw attention to your use of the past tense to show that the event has happened.

Real events

Learn

How do I write about real events?

Real events include: school trips, holidays, a birthday party or a disaster (like an earthquake).

There of lots of others!

Start by planning your writing:

What is the event?	Our day out.
Who was there?	Oak Class, Rowan Class and teachers.
What happened first?	We got on the bus.
Describe an interesting or exciting part.	Jamie got lost and we didn't know know where he was.
How did the event end?	He was found near the fairground.

Make brief notes to remind you of what you want to say.
When you are writing, remember to show what **punctuation** you can use.

commas in list • capital letters for a person's name

Our day out

The bus came early and Oak Class, Rowan Class, Mr Beech and Mrs Maple got on. Mr Beech's class went upstairs and we were downstairs. How long would it take to get there? It was very exciting! After an hour the bus slowed down and we arrived. We couldn't wait to get off.

apostrophe for possession

question and question mark

exclamation and exclamation mark

apostrophe for missing letter

There is a clear description of how the day started. We know who is going on the day out. We know the children are excited, but we don't know where they have gone or what they will do.

- Tell the children to use the plan to write about their event. Ensure that they have enough time to talk and plan before they write. Encourage them to tell their sentences to their partner before they write them down.

- The textbook has an annotated example for planning and writing about an event. Children can then use the planning and prompts on the activity page to plan and write about something that has happened to them. There is a list of tips that the children can refer to so that their writing makes sense and has accurate punctuation.

- Use the templates in *100 English Lessons Year 2* and the *Year 2 Practice Book* to plan their ideas before writing.

Activities

1. **Finish writing about the rest of the day out. You can use some of the notes from page 72 and you may need to make up events.**
   Describe:
   - Where the children have gone.
   - What they did.
   - What exciting things happened. Remember to use interesting adjectives and adverbs.
   - Whether it was a good day out or a disastrous day.

   ### ✓ Tip

   Use capital letters to start a sentence and for people's names, place names, days of the week and months.

   Write different types of sentences and use question marks and exclamation marks.

   Use commas in lists.

   Use apostrophes for missing letters or for possession.

2. **Now think of a real event that you have taken part in. Plan what you will put in your account.**
   - What was the event?
   - Who was there?
   - What made it fun, interesting or terrible?
   - Did you learn anything or were there any problems?
   - How did it end?

   Always read your finished writing. Check: Does it make sense? Have I repeated something? Is it interesting?

   Share your ideas with a partner. Ask each other questions about the events. Finally write about your real event, using interesting verbs, adverbs and adjectives.

   Writing **73**

100 English Lessons Year 2 links:

- Spring 1, Week 3 (pages 89–91): write a recount
- Spring 1, Week 5 (pages 95–97): write an information guide
- Summer 1, Week 3 (pages 153–155): write a leaflet

Year 2 Practice Book links:

- (page 123): What happened and when?

Poetry

Prior learning

- Read poems.
- Terminology: rhyme, rhythm, line, stanza or verse.

Learn

- Make sure the children have read and discussed a variety of poems before writing.
- Collect ideas from the poems that you have read together and create a list of words, phrases and images that the children can refer to when they write poems.

- It is easy to write a poem with a simple structure. Show children a kenning – this is a poem where each line is made up of two nouns joined together to describe the qualities of something. Kennings come from Viking poetry where the sea is described with the kenning 'whale road'.

Many kennings have a noun ending in 'er' as the second word, so a cat might be described as a 'mouse catcher', 'sunlight snoozer' or 'daytime dreamer'. Tell the children they are going to write a kenning about something they are very familiar with, such as a pet, a family member, a teacher, snow.

Curriculum objectives

- To write poetry.
- To plan or say out loud what they are going to write about.
- To write down ideas and/ or keywords, including new vocabulary.
- To encapsulate what they want to say, line by line.

Success criteria

- I can think carefully about my word choices when I write a poem.

Poetry

How do I write poetry?

Learn

Poetry is writing where feelings and ideas are described with interesting words, often using rhyme and rhythm. Some poems rhyme, but they don't have to.

It is cold is not very interesting. When writing a poem, you need to add adjectives and cut out words that are not needed.

The freezing hail clattering on the glass tells us more about the cold and gives some description.

Choose a topic to write your poem about. Then make a list of nouns and adjectives or verbs about that topic, for example **winter**.

Nouns	Adjectives or verbs
frost	freezing
snow	glistening
hail	floating
cold	fluttering
ice	shiny
icicle	sharp

Use your list to help you start writing.

Freezing snow fluttering down

How is it fluttering? ← Can I add an adverb?

Freezing snow fluttering softly down.

Could I use a different adverb?

Freezing snow fluttering silently down.

You could make some lines rhyme.
Snow and glow rhyme. Nose and toes rhyme.
It can be tricky getting these words to the end of a line!

- Collect nouns and 'er' nouns that are associated with that thing and write them on the board. Model joining the two nouns to create a kenning, then build your poem by making a few of these. Ask the children to write their own kennings as a group. First, give them ten or so sticky notes and tell them to write a noun on each one. Then give them a second set of different coloured sticky notes to write the 'er' nouns on.

Tell the children to make kennings by pairing a noun and an 'er' noun. They can play around with the order and add new words until they are happy with their creation.

- Ensure the children understand that writing good poetry relies on choosing the best words not necessarily the most fancy ones, and that poems need not be long. Sometimes a simple word is the best word, and a short poem can be the most profound!

Activities

- The textbook shows how careful word choices create vivid imagery in poems. Children can practise using the prompts to write a poem about autumn.

- There are many ideas about how to use poems in *100 English Lessons Year 2*.

- Use the poetry ideas in the *Year 2 Practice Book* to scaffold children's writing.

Activities

1. a. Write three lines of poetry about winter. Use the nouns and adjectives about winter, from page 74. Make sure you use nouns, adjectives and adverbs.

   b. Now write another three lines of poetry about winter, using your own words this time.

> **✓ Tip**
>
> Think about something you really like about winter – perhaps a snowman or the outline of a tree.

2. Write a poem about autumn. First make a list of nouns and adjectives about autumn. Now add a list of adverbs you could use. Decide what you want to say about autumn.

   You could think about:

   - leaves   - colours   - the weather   - clothes

   Share your ideas with a partner. Use your lists to make different lines about autumn. Discuss which lines work best. Could you improve a line by changing or adding some words?

   Finally, try writing some lines. Look at them.

   - Do they need more adjectives or adverbs?
   - Are there extra words that you don't need?
   - Do your lines say what you want to say about autumn?

> **✓ Tip**
>
> Try playing with different ways of saying something, until you find the best way.
>
> Can you change any lines in your poem so that they rhyme?

Writing **75**

100 English Lessons Year 2 links:

- Autumn 1, Week 6 (pages 34–36): write an alphabetical list poem

- Spring 1, Week 6 (pages 98–100): plan and write a list poem

- Spring 2, Week 6 (pages 130–132): acrostic poem

- Summer 1, Week 2 (pages 150–152): write a poem using noun phrases

- Summer 2, Week 3 (pages 185–187): write a poem

Year 2 Practice Book links:

- (page 124): Write a poem
- (page 125): Sounds of the city

Writing for different purposes

Prior learning

- Can read a range of different non-fiction writing.
- Understand that writing has to reflect its purpose and intended audience.

Learn

- Gather examples of different types of writing used in the school, such as letters, leaflets, maps, posters and instructions. Look at them together and discuss who their audience is and what purpose they have. Look at each example in turn and draw out how the writing is organised and how the layout suits the purpose. For instance, a poster is best suited to giving information quickly: it should have writing large enough to be read at a distance and short enough to be read quickly.

- Give the children imaginary writing tasks to consider, such as to tell other schoolchildren about healthy food, and ask them to select the best format. Encourage them to give reasons for their choices and help them think about how best to appeal to their audience.
- When you set writing tasks, ensure that the purpose and audience is clear. Model planning your writing, showing the children how you think about the tone. Explain that a very formal tone with fancy language would be inappropriate on a poster addressed to children, and that slang would not be right in a letter to a parent!
- Ensure the children have enough time to talk and plan before they write.

Curriculum objectives

- To write for different purposes.
- To plan or say out loud what they are going to write about.
- To write down ideas and/or keywords, including new vocabulary.
- To encapsulate what they want to say, sentence by sentence.

Success criteria

- I can write for different purposes.
- I can include all the main facts/information.
- I can decide which type of writing suits my purpose best.
- I can choose the best layout for my writing.

Writing for different purposes

What is writing for different purposes?

Learn

Writing is used for many different purposes:

A letter

Dear Mrs Bond,

I am writing to ask if we could have more toys in our playground. Sometimes it is boring at playtime and if we have a variety of equipment, children would play together and learn more.

Thank you for reading this letter.

Yours sincerely,
Asha

A poster

Friday 26 February 2016

Robin Hood

at St Andrew's Church Hall.
7:30pm

Adults £3.00 Children £1.50

Instructions

How to clean your teeth

You need:
toothpaste, toothbrush and water

What to do:
1. First put toothpaste on your brush.
2. Next spend at least 2 minutes brushing the top and bottom of your teeth.
3. Finally rinse your mouth with the water.

A report

Sports Day took place on Wednesday afternoon.

It was a beautiful sunny afternoon, though a little hot for the runners.

There were several events, including 100 metre running, a relay and the egg and spoon race. The most popular event was the sack race, which was very amusing to watch.

Bowland House won the team prize.

How many other different purposes can you think of for writing?

Look at the types of writing above. What differences can you see in the way they are organised?

- What tense is each one written in?
- Are they all written in sentences?
- Do any use numbers?
- Do they all start and finish in the same way?
- What essential information does each one need to include?

Activities

- Use the textbook to recap children's understanding of writing for different purposes. Discuss how the language and layout used reflect the purpose of the writing. Use the writing activities to inspire children to write independently for different purposes. Can they make their writing suit the purpose and cover all the information required?

- *100 English Lessons Year 2* covers a wide range of writing types and purposes including leaflets, maps, recounts, instructions and factfiles.

Activities

1. **Write a thank-you letter, to say thank you for a birthday present.**

   Think about:
   - Who you are writing to.
   - How you start and finish your letter.
   - What was the present? What did you like about it?
   - Something interesting you could say about your birthday.
   - Whether your letter will be in sentences or in numbered points.

2. **Write a report about a trip you have been on.**

   Talk to a partner about the following:
   - Where was the trip to and how did you get there?
   - What did you like or not like?
   - Who did you go with?
   - Will your report be written in the present or past tense?

   When you have shared your ideas with a partner, write the report. Remember to read your report to make sure it makes sense.

3. **Choose something you have made in technology or art. Write instructions on how to make it.**

   Think about:
   - What you need.
   - How you will organise the instructions: in sentences or numbered points?
   - What you did first, next, finally.

   Ask a partner to read your instructions. Do they make sense? Have you missed anything out?

Writing **77**

Editing

Prior learning

- Understand and use the simple present and past tenses.
- Understand and use the progressive present and past tenses.

Learn

- Ensure that children read their work and identify which parts of it they are pleased with or feel are particularly successful before you begin the editing process.
- Read the children's work, looking for common errors. These are likely to be a lack of pronoun cohesion, lack of subject-verb agreement, inconsistency in verb tense, lack of determiners, incomplete verb structures and inaccurate or weak verb choices. Choose one or two types of error and use these to model the editing process. Write a text with the same purpose as the children's writing, and containing similar errors, on a flipchart or board. Ask the children to read the text and identify any mistakes they can find. Underline the errors. Then ask the children to help you correct the mistakes.

Curriculum objectives

- To re-read to check that their writing makes sense and that verbs to indicate time are used correctly and consistently, including verbs in the progressive form.

Success criteria

- I can edit my writing so the verbs are used correctly.
- I can edit my writing so that it makes sense.

Explain your thinking as you do this and focus on how the writing improves with these corrections. Change weak verbs for more accurate ones and make over-long noun phrases more compact by improving the word choices. Check that you are meeting the purpose of the text. Read your work back and ask the children to tell you why it is better now.

- Ask the children to work with a partner to identify any similar mistakes in their writing and fix them. Choose other types of error and repeat this process.

Editing

What is editing?

Learn

When we edit writing, we check it to see if there are any mistakes and to see if we can improve it. Read this text.

> It is a sunny day and we went for a long walk. It took us a long time and we were very tired. It started to get dark and we was frightened.

Check:

1. **Does it make sense?**

   It **is** a sunny day and we **went** for a long walk.
   ↑ present tense   ↑ past tense

   The tense should stay the same, so change all the verbs to the past tense.

   It **was** a sunny day and we **went** for a long walk.

2. **Are there any mistakes?**

   we **was** very frightened   we **were** very frightened
   ↑
   is not Standard English

3. **Is there any repetition?**

   Every sentence starts with **It**. So change some of them.

   Today was a sunny day   **As** it started to get dark...

4. **Could I make it more interesting?**

   ...we went for a **long** walk. It took us a **long** time and we **were** tired.

   long is repeated – use a more interesting adjective: **exhausting**.
   became is a more interesting verb than **were**.

78   Writing

- Put children in pairs to read each other's work aloud. The child whose work it is has an editing pen and marks their text when they hear that a word is missing, or if they think that something doesn't sound right. When their work has been read, tell the children to talk about the text. Does the child who was reading have any feedback for their partner? Ask the children to work together to fix any obvious errors such as capital letters, full stops and missing words. Then ask them to swap roles and repeat the activity so both partners' work is read and edited.

Activities

- The textbook explains some common errors that children will find in their work and shows how to correct them. There is a piece of text for them to practise editing.
- Editing is embedded in the writing process throughout *100 English Lessons Year 2*.

---

5. Now read the edited text.

Today was a sunny day and we went for an exhausting walk. It took us a long time and we became tired. As it started to get dark we were very frightened.

Activities

I. **The text below needs editing. Read it with a partner.**

a. Make a list of the mistakes you find.

The pantomime are well attended. The audience were very enthusiastic about the show and clapt loud. widow twanky make them laugh until we cryed.

b. Now rewrite it, by yourself, correcting all the mistakes.

c. Can you find any other ways to improve this text?

2. **Now list all the mistakes in this text. Rewrite it, correctly.**

The iland of Anglesey were off the north-west coast of Wales. You can drive to anglesey over the Menai Suspension Bridge. There was many beautiful beach and even South Stack Lighthouse, were you will see puffins. Sum people drove across Anglesey so they can caught the ferry to Ireland.

3. **Choose your own piece of writing. Read it carefully, looking for mistakes.**

- List any mistakes and any repetition.
- Can you use more interesting verbs, adjectives or adverbs?
- Discuss your writing with a partner. Can they suggest ways to improve it?
- Now rewrite your piece, correcting mistakes and adding any improvements.

✓ **Tip**

It must make sense.
Use the same tense.
Avoid repetition.
Make it interesting.

Writing **79**

100 English Lessons Year 2 links:

- Autumn 2, Week 3 (page 59): Lesson 5, Checking and reading aloud
- Autumn 2, Week 4 (page 62): Lesson 5, Games day
- Autumn 2, Week 5 (page 65): Lesson 5, Building diary memories
- Spring 1, Week 3 (page 91): Lesson 4, Writing a recount
- Spring 2, Assess and review (page 135): Checking, proofreading and correcting
- Summer 2, Week 2 (page 184): Lesson 5, Ship's log display
- Summer 2, Week 6 (pages 194–196): re-read stories with a focus on punctuation

Proofreading

Prior learning

- Can write and edit own work.

Learn

- Proofreading happens after the children have edited their work and concentrates on accurate use of spelling, grammar, punctuation and Standard English.
- Read the children's edited work, looking for inaccuracies in these areas. Common inaccuracies include past tense verbs spelled with 'd' and 't' instead of 'ed', lack of capital letters for proper nouns, incorrect use of pronouns ('he' and 'she' mixed up), lack of commas in lists and sentences not demarcated.
- Write a text with some of the errors you have found. Ask the children to help you underline your inaccuracies. Ask them to spell misspelled words for you. Make the changes in your work for spelling, then ask the children to work in pairs to do the same with their work. Repeat the process for inaccuracies in grammar, punctuation and Standard English.

Activities

- The textbook explains some common errors that children will find in their work and shows how to correct them.
- Proofreading is embedded in the writing process throughout *100 English Lessons Year 2*.

Curriculum objectives

- To proofread to check for errors in spelling, grammar and punctuation.

Success criteria

- I can find errors in my writing and correct them.

100 English Lessons Year 2 links:

- Autumn 1, Week 4 (pages 28–30): re-read writing to check spelling, grammar and punctuation
- Autumn 2, Week 3 (pages 57–59): proofread the first draft of their own story
- Spring 1, Week 3 (pages 89–91): re-read and proofread own recounts to check for sense
- Spring 2, Assess and review (pages 135): Checking, proofreading and correcting
- Summer 1, Week 6 (pages 162–164): proofread and edit own stories
- Summer 2, Week 2 (pages 182–184): re-read ship's log for sense and proofread

---

Proofreading

Learn

What is proofreading?

When you are proofreading you read your writing to check for mistakes. There might be mistakes in:

- spelling
- punctuation
- grammar
- Standard English.

Look at this story:

> Once upon a time, there were a beautiful girl. She was called cinderella. One day they were all invitd to a ball which would be held in the palis. How excited they were.

- Spelling mistakes:
  they were all invitd ➔ past tense is verb + ed = invited
  held in the palis. ➔ use a dictionary to find correct spelling = palace
- Punctuation mistakes:
  cinderella ➔ names of people start with a capital letter = Cinderella
  How excited they were. ➔ exclamation = How excited they were!
- Grammar or Standard English mistake:
  there were a beautiful girl.
  ➔ only one girl, so a singular verb = there was a beautiful girl.

Activities

1. **Proofread this text to find the mistakes. Make a list of all the mistakes you can find. Then rewrite the text correctly.**

   > I could here creaking on the stairs. It is very scary. I did'nt know what are making that noyse. What should I do!

Answers Year 2

GRAMMATICAL WORDS

Page 6

1 a. I dug the <u>garden</u> with a <u>spade</u>.
   b. I ate <u>pasta</u> with a <u>fork</u>.

2 a. I walked through the dark **night**.
   b. It was a cold, snowy **day**.

Page 7

1 a. We gave out homework to <u>Mr Patel</u>.
   b. Our class go swimming every <u>Tuesday</u>.

2 a. I am going to <u>menorca</u> for my holiday.
   b. My birthday is in <u>february</u>.
   c. <u>preston</u> is on the <u>river ribble</u>.

Page 8

1 a. They had a <u>short</u> walk home.
   b. A <u>gigantic</u> parcel arrived this morning.

2 Accept any appropriate adjective, for example:
   a. At last they found the **old** treasure chest.
   b. We couldn't wait to arrive at the **ruined** castle.

Page 9

1 a. It was an <u>interesting book</u>.
   b. The train took us on a <u>long, boring journey</u>.

2 Accept any appropriate noun phrases, for example:
   a **large**, **fierce** lion; the **long**, **scaly** snake

Page 10

1 a. Jack <u>draws</u> a picture of a train.
   b. They <u>eat</u> their sandwiches hungrily.

2 a. We look in the shops for a football.
   b. She watches a very scary film.

Page 11

1

Present tense	Past tense
we clean	we **cleaned**
I **help**	I helped
he talks	he **talked**
they **push**	they pushed

2 a. We **pulled** the rope onto the boat.
   b. She **ate** her meal slowly.

Page 12

1 a. Ellie **is** washing her hair tonight.
   b. Auntie Kath and Uncle Richard **are** taking me to the cinema.
   c. I **am** eating my tea.

2 a. am walking b. are blowing

3 a. We are going to the pool. b. I am swimming backstroke.

Page 13

1 Accept any appropriate verb + 'ing', for example:
   a. The children were **building** sandcastles.
   b. Jane was **riding** her bike.
   c. I was **watching** television.

2 Accept any appropriate verb, written in the past progressive,
   for example:
   a. The boy was drinking. b. The man (He) was kicking a ball.
   c. The woman (lady/She) was driving a car. d. The girl was skipping.
   e. The children (They) were playing catch. f. The girl was painting.

Page 15

1 a. quietly b. greedily c. happily d. heavily

2 a. I walked <u>slowly</u> to school in the rain.
   b. My friend was <u>happily</u> talking to her mum.
   c. The snow fell <u>silently</u> onto the garden.

3 The birds sang **noisily** as the sun rose in the sky.

4 Accept any appropriate adverb.

Page 16

1 a. I dropped the plate **and** the mug.
   b. I wanted an egg **but** there were none left.

2 We could go to the zoo **or** we could go on a boat trip.

Page 17

1 a. It was after dark <u>when</u> the owl began to hoot.
   b. <u>If</u> the car needs petrol, we will need to stop.

2 Accept either **when** in both or **because**.

Page 19

1 a. I go to school every day.
   b. They are helping me to do my homework.
   c. The cat was drinking her milk greedily. **or** The cats were drinking
      their milk greedily.

2 a. would of
      right dear
   b. He would have loved to go on the trip but it was too dear/
      expensive.

3 a. Mum and Dad were making our tea.
   b. Harry should have cleaned the rabbit's cage.

4 Review the examples of non-Standard English and the standard
   equivalents.

PUNCTUATION

Page 20

1 a. Why did you go to the shops?   question
   b. It is a new house.   statement
   c. The dog is very muddy.   statement
   d. Who wants a drink?   question

Page 21

1 a. Go home **command**
   b. How much has it grown **question**
   c. How clever you are **exclamation**
   d. It was planted last week **statement**

2 a. Go home.
   b. How much has it grown**?**
   c. How clever you are**!**
   d. It was planted last week**.**

Page 22

1 a. I have a sandwich, yoghurt, crisps and a drink in my lunch box.
   b. September, April, June and November all have thirty days.
   c. He washed all the mugs, bowls, plates and spoons.
   d. They did maths, science, art and PE on Monday.

Page 23

2 My grandparents, cousins, aunts and uncles all came to my party.

3 Accept any combination of four of the items in each list.

4 Accept any sentence which lists four friends with commas in the
   correct place.

5 Accept any sentence which lists four favourite foods with commas
   in the correct place.

6 Accept any sentence which lists four favourite hobbies with
   commas in the correct place.

Page 24

1 a. I **haven't** finished my lunch.
   b. We **can't** reach it.
   c. The children **weren't** enjoying the pantomime.
   d. **You'll** have to pay for the tickets now.

Page 25

2 a. I have b. does not c. they are d. what is or what has
   e. was not f. could have

3 a. It is b. It will c. I would d. He had

4 **a.** I am = I'm
   b. they were not = they weren't
   c. we did not = we didn't
   d. he would = he'd
   e. they have = they've

5 Review the children's answers.

1 **a.** We were woken up by the baby's crying.
   b. I enjoyed playing with Maya's game.
   c. The footballer's goal was very exciting.
   d. They were reading their favourite author's latest novel.

2 **a.** The cat's food had been eaten.
   b. The cake's filling was delicious.

3 **a.** the book belongs to Jamie
   b. the roof belongs to the house
   c. the neck belongs to the giraffe
   d. the pen belongs to Miss Woodworth

4 **a.** Accept any combination of people and objects, one object for each person.
   b. Accept any appropriate sentence.

VOCABULARY

Page 29

1 amaze**ment** hand**ful** penni**less** fond**ness**

2 move**ment** tearful/tearless hopeless/hopeful sad**ness**

3 happi**ness** merri**ment** penni**less** beautiful

4 Accept any sentences which use the words in question 3 appropriately.

5 strong**ly** soft**ly** quick**ly** safe**ly**

6 angri**ly** busi**ly** hungri**ly** easi**ly**

7 Accept any two sentences which use any of the new adverbs appropriately.

8 Accept any appropriate adverbs, for example:

Verb	Adverb
climb	carefully
read	enthusiastically
swim	strongly

9 'ly'

Page 30

1 higher, highest
   hotter, hottest
   heavier, heaviest
   wider, widest

2 cleaner builder baker

Page 31

1 nod, **nodded**, **nodding**
   jump, **jumped**, **jumping**
   study, **studied**, **studying**
   joke, **joked**, **joking**
   cry, **cried**, **crying**

Page 32

1 **a.** ques**tion** ac**tion** addi**tion**
   b. Accept sentences which use the above words appropriately.

2 I caught a train from the **station**.
   We entered the **competition** and won a day at the theme park.
   The class are learning **subtraction** of pairs of two-digit numbers.
   The car's **motion** made him feel ill.

3 Review the children's answers.

SPELLING

Page 33

1 **a.** W**e** went to the b**ea**ch to s**ee** the sand.
   b. The ch**ie**f raised the gr**ee**n flag comp**le**t**e**ly.

2 **a.** fright **b.** cube **c.** shield

1 **a.** My teacher **taught** me about Florence Nightingale.
   b. Dinosaurs lived millions of years ago.
   c. My little sister has begun to **crawl**.
   d. I cuddle my teddy **bear** in bed.
   e. We picked **pears** off the tree.

Page 35

1 wasp
   waffle

2 **a.** I **want** a drink, please.
   b. Go and **wash** your hands and face.
   c. Ali was in the football **squad** for this season's games.
   d. You will need to **squash** the boxes before putting them in the bin.
   e. My **watch** says it is ten o'clock.

3 **a.** a crouching position – squat
   b. something of value – quality
   c. argument – quarrel
   d. a number of things – quantity

Page 36

1 **a.** squirrel
   b. camel
   c. capital

2 Accept any appropriate sentences using each of the above words.

Page 37

2 **a.** The baby's **bottle** was full of milk.
   b. The train went through the dark **tunnel**.
   c. They collected a very old **fossil** from the seashore.
   d. We had to **pedal** hard to get our bikes up the hill.

3 **a.** al: hospital, animal
      el: tunnel, camel, towel, tinsel, travel
      il: pencil, nostril, fossil
      le: apple, middle, table
   b. Accept any appropriate words belonging to each group.

4 Check words with the endings 'al', 'el', 'il', or 'le' have been found.

Page 38

1 ledge ✓ page badge ✓ charge dodge ✓

2 **a.** stage **b.** large **c.** strange **d.** judge

Page 39

1 **w**rite **k**nob **g**naw **k**nife

2 To use needles and wool to make clothes – **knit**
   A ship at the bottom of the sea – **wreck/shipwreck**
   To chew – **gnaw**

Page 40

1 soft c: spicy, cinema, pencil
   not soft c: camel, picture, camera, camping

2 **a.** The curry was very sp**icy**.
   b. My pen**cil** needs sharpening.
   c. She will need to take a spoon of medi**cine** three times daily.
   d. Every sent**ence** starts with a capital letter.

Page 41

1 Accept any appropriate examples with the ending 'sion' or 'sure'.

2 confu**sion**
   plea**sure**
   divi**sion**
   mea**sure**
   in**sure**
   explo**sion**
   un**sure**
   deci**sion**

Page 42

1 cry, shy, try, sly

2 spy, fly, July, sky, tie, lie, die multiply

Page 43

1 A herb – parsley   It is often eaten at Christmas – turkey
   A trip – journey   It is used to put shopping in – trolley
   Organ in the body – kidney   Land between hills – valley
   Bees make it – honey

2 **a.** I have been saving **money** to buy a new game.
 b. **Monkeys** live in hot countries and can be very naughty.
 c. The **jockey** rode the horse fast over the jumps.
 d. There was smoke coming out of the **chimney**.

Page 44

1 call, fall, gall, hall, tall, wall; also stall, small

2 **a.** After a long **walk** we needed to clean our muddy boots.
 b. Our dog has just had three **small** puppies.
 c. As the sun went down we waited for **nightfall**.
 d. The children put their swimming things into a large **holdall**.
 e. We **all** read every evening after tea.

Page 45

1 month, brother, loves, come, mother, covers, lovely, done, some

2 **a.** Short /u/ sound before 'n': money, month, front, monkey
  Short /u/ sound before 'v': love, above, govern, cover, dove
  Short /u/ sound before 'th': nothing, another
 b. some, dozen
  Accept any appropriate sentences using any of above words.

Page 46

1 warden   warmest   warped   wardrobe

2 **a.** Europe has sent some **warships** to the Mediterranean Sea.
 b. The lighthouse **warns** ships that they are near rocks.
 c. The **warden** in the Nature Reserve showed us how to pond dip.
 d. We enjoyed the sun's **warmth** as we played on the beach.

3 Accept any four sentences which use the given words appropriately.

Page 47

1 A male who does a job – workman
 The Earth and everything on it – world
 A piece of paper with tasks on it – worksheet
 A long creature which lives in soil – worm
 A group of letters with meaning – word

2 **a.** wor**k**ers, wa**r**ning, wo**r**se, awa**r**ded, wo**r**med/wa**r**med, wo**r**ldly, wo**r**ship/wa**r**ship, wo**r**ked
 b. Accept any appropriate sentence using any of above words.

3 **a.** word, wormed, workforce, worshipped, worn, worsen
 b. worn

Page 48

1 **a.** friend + ly   **b.** be + hind   **c.** im + prove   **d.** peop + le

2 **a.** friendly – making short /e/ sound
 b. behind – 'ind'
 c. improve – 'o–e' making /oo/ sound
 d. people – 'eo' to make 'ee' sound, 'le' at the end

3 Accept any appropriate sentence using each word, for example:
 a. I wanted to play tennis but the others wanted to play cricket.
 b. We were allowed to stay up late because it was Friday.
 c. Sophie fell into a puddle and her clothes were really muddy!

Page 49

1 tooth — fish
 rain — glasses
 sun — brush
 jelly — coat

2 Accept any appropriate compound word, for example:
 a. moon**light**   **b.** wheel**barrow**   **c.** tea**spoon**   **d.** bed**room**

Page 50

1 **a.** Look over there!
 b. Have you wrapped their presents?
 c. I don't know if they're here yet.

Page 51

1 **a.** There is a **sale** on in our local bike shop.
 b. Jack went to **meet** his friend.
 c. The dog hurt his **paw**.

2 Accept any answer using each word, for example:
 a. The **sun** is very hot.
 b. His **son** is good at rugby.

Page 53

1 Singular: window, kiss, **church**, **flower**, **toe**
 Plural: **windows**, **kisses**, churches, flowers, toes

2 **a.** trays **b.** ladies **c.** lorries **d.** keys
 e. flies
 f. berries

3 **a.** Lots of **turkeys** are sold at Christmas.
 b. We walked through several **valleys** before reaching the village.
 c. Some **countries** are often hot.

4 **a.** cities
 b. butterflies
 c. families
 d. monkeys

5 Change the 'y' to 'i' and add 'es', but if there is a vowel before the 'y', just add 's'.

READING

Page 54

1 Some of the children started running around near Ralf.
 Ralf held his mother's hand tightly.
 The teacher met them at the door.

Page 55

1 They were more difficult **or** she had to learn by using the easier things first **or** the balls were too easy.

Page 57

1 headings, subheadings

2 headings: what the whole piece of writing is about
 subheadings: what a part of the writing is about
 numbers: the order things are done
 bullet points: what is needed, but not the order

3 Shopping list

4 Accept any answer which mentions order, for example:
 Because the order you do things in is important.

Page 59

1 fiercely

2 ripped

3 quickly (or a word with a similar meaning)

Page 60

1 Accept any of the following:
 Nasreen is very funny.
 She makes everyone laugh.
 Everyone is happy when Nasreen is there.

2 Because it was quiet.

Page 61

1 Tigers can run fast and have sharp claws and teeth.

Page 62

1 going very fast on her bike.
 She needed to stop quickly.
 There was a loud snap
 her front brake fell off!

Page 63

2 Accept any reasonable answer, for example: She will not stop. She will crash. She will manage to stop.

3 Accept any reasonable answer that explains the choices, for example: She will crash because she cannot control her bike. She will manage to stop because she scrapes her shoes on the road.

4 Encourage your child to explain how they came to their predictions.

5 Accept any reasonable answer that explains the choices, for example:

What could happen next?	Why?
1. The ambulance crew takes Lorna to hospital.	She could have crashed into the car.
2. The ambulance crew takes the car driver to hospital.	The car could have crashed trying to avoid Lorna.
3. The ambulance drives past because it is for someone else.	Lorna was very lucky and missed the car.

6 Accept any reasonable answer that explains the choices, for example: Police because there has been an accident; newspaper reporters because they want to write an article about the crash.

7 Accept any reasonable answer that explains their thoughts, for example: The car driver will visit Lorna in hospital because he wants to know that she is all right.

8 Accept answers that follow the clues in the text and have realistic endings.

Page 65

1 a. It has fallen out of Ethan's pocket.
   b. It fell out of his pocket through the hole.

2 hungrily

3 bravely

4 Feeling: Accept any reasonable answers, for example: happy.
   Reasons: Accept any two reasonable answers that follow on from the feeling, for example:
   It was her birthday.
   She had a present.
   It was just what she wanted.
   She wasn't disappointed.

Page 67

1 a. Stalk – a part of a plant.
      Hovering – staying in one place in the air.
   b. *No toad spy you* means that you do not see a toad.
   c. Accept any reasonable answers with reasons, for example:
      I liked the rhymes because they made it sound interesting.
   d. The caterpillar becomes a chrysalis and then turns into a butterfly.
      Children may not know the word *chrysalis* or be aware of that stage.
   e. Any reasonable questions are acceptable.

Page 69

1 a. pink, brink; red, bed; blue, through; white, light; yellow, mellow; green, between
   b. violet and twilight
   c. Accept any reasonable answer to do with rhyme, for example:
      It's very hard to find a rhyme for orange.

2 There are lots of things! Accept any of the repeated parts with the owl, the snake or the fox. Accept any of the repeated phrases.

3 Repeated: I didn't want.
   Rhymes: kite, height; try, cry.

WRITING

Page 70

1 Accept any non-fiction writing which is written appropriately.

Page 71

1 Accept any story which is written appropriately about a pet.

Page 73

1 Accept any ending which is written accurately and:
   • describes where the children have gone
   • what they did there
   • describes what happened when Jamie got lost and how he was found

2 Accept any account of a real event which is written accurately and:
   • is clearly described, with a clear beginning and end
   • tells what the events is and who took part
   • describes what made it interesting/terrible

Page 75

1 a. Accept any three lines of poetry about winter, using given and other words. Do not accept sentences about winter. Children should make use of adjectives and adverbs. The lines do not need to rhyme.
   b. As above, but children should use their own words about winter. The lines do not need to rhyme.

2 Children should first write a list of nouns, adjectives and adverbs which could be used in an autumn poem. These and other words should be used to write a few lines of poetry about autumn. The lines do not need to rhyme.

Page 77

1 Accept any thank-you letter which should is written accurately.

2 Accept any report about a trip which is written accurately.

3 Accept any instructions about how to make something which is written accurately.

Page 79

1 a. The pantomime **are** well attended. The audience **were** very enthusiastic about the show and **clapt loud. widow twanky** made them laugh until **we cryed.**
   b. The pantomime **was** well attended. The audience **was** very enthusiastic about the show and **clapped loudly. Widow Twanky** made them laugh until **they cried.**
   c. Accept any appropriate sentences.

2 The **island** of Anglesey **is** off the north-west coast of Wales. You can drive to **Anglesey** over the Menai Suspension Bridge. There **are** many beautiful **beaches** and even South Stack Lighthouse, **where** you will see puffins. **Some** people **drive** across Anglesey so they can **catch** the ferry to Ireland.

3 Review children's revisions.

Page 80

1 I could **hear** creaking on the stairs. It **was** very scary. I **didn't** know what **was** making that **noise.** What should I do**?**